Winning GOLF

David W. Smith

Winning at GOLF

David W. Smith

STARBURST PUBLISHERS

P.O. Box 4123, Lancaster, Pennsylvania 17604

To schedule Author appearances write:
Author Appearances, Starburst Promotions, P.O. Box 4123
Lancaster, Pennsylvania 17604 or call (717) 293-0939

Credits:
Cover design by Terry Dugan
Illustrations by Dwain Skinner

WINNING AT GOLF

First Printing, April 1995

ISBN: 0-914984-46-2
Library of Congress Catalog Number 92-81394

Printed in the United States of America

To

Bert, Autumn, Aaron, Family and *Friends*

**After all David, you haven't failed . . .
you just haven't succeeded."**—Buck White

Acknowledgements

This book is dedicated to the three men I admire most:

My father (H. Allen Smith, Jr.)— a man's man, larger than life, and my own personal John Wayne;

General George S. Patton— to whom all of the free world owes their profound gratitude and admiration;

Mr. Buck White— who is responsible for my outlook on golf and who made this book possible.

Buck White

H. A. Smith, Jr.

General Patton

My father passed away on October 18, 1980. If I saw him today I would say, "Daddy, did you know that you're my hero . . . and everything I'd like to be." When I think of my father it gives my heart a smile, my face lights up, and I think . . . I can't help but make it. I am reminded of what an awesome responsibility we have as humans, to be the best we can be. When the "roll" is called, let it show that . . . "we showed up for life."

As I think of Mr. White I am reminded that as golfers what a great privilege and obligation we have as custodians of the game and torchbearers, to carry the torch that symbolizes all those who have gone before us, to pass along to the next generation the love of the game, and to preserve its integrity.

When I think of General Patton I am reminded of how one man, believing in himself, helped change the world.

Let us all remember it was not intended that we go it alone. We live in a world of turmoil, one of trying times, of great pressures. It is not good to think too highly of ourselves; our fortunes, our accomplishments, and well being; because in judging and criticizing others we may be reminded of this, "But for the grace of God, There go I." We all are in need of a shepherd. Evangelist Dr. Angel Martinez said it best in his sermon entitled *The Living Shepherd,* "The 23rd Psalm is the philosophy of life set to music. The scholars contend that David wrote the 23rd Psalm. I believe I could have written it—David just beat me to it. Because the 23rd Psalm is the sincere expression of every person who knows the Lord, the risen Lord. And the reason why this Psalm is so popular is because David took the words right out of our mouths. He said what you and I would say as to what constitutes God's leadership on the level of everyday human experience."

Every day I live I realize God has blessed my life and I have found favor in his eyes. Surely, I have enjoyed life as much as anyone has a right to. I believe that one day God looked at the problems of this world and determined that man needed encouragement and hope. So He made fathers. Then, realizing life was still too complex, He reached down into the bottom of his heart and made mothers. Thank God for mothers. In one last attempt to show His generosity, God said, I am going to give man fellowship with people that will be more valuable than gold or silver. So God made "friends." And contrary to what you may hear, there are absolutes. There is right and wrong. Life is still worth living and God has not changed sides . . . . He's still where He's always been . . . on His throne in Heaven.

David Wayne Smith

Contents

Preface

In this book, I have attempted to put into words my education as a golfer . . . both in instruction and in application . . . as told to me by one Emmitt O'Neal "Buck" White, born February 9, 1911, and died January 23, 1982. I hope that you will enjoy the similarities in teachings I have tried to parallel between Mr. White and General George S. Patton. In some instances, when I thought my own words were inadequate, I have tried to insert quotes from other great golfers. Make no mistake about it. My sole ability to seek out such information was guided by what I learned from Mr. White. Without his guidance, I would have been like the little boy who stumbled up to the four-way intersection, confused as to the path he should go. He did not know which direction he should choose. He also did not know where he had been. My purpose is to pass along this knowledge and lore to those who have the desire to learn and will benefit from that knowledge. In Mr. White's absence, I have attempted to interpret and communicate his teachings in a way that will cause you to feel that you have experienced them.

May I go on record as saying I believe anyone who really wants to can learn to play golf and play it well. I offer this encouragement to all. Dispel any thoughts you may have with regards to good players being born with this knowledge. It isn't so!

Do not be not discouraged. Through desire, hard work, determination, practice, correct instruction, and application anyone can play well. "By perseverance, and study, and eternal desire, any man can become great."–General Patton

I realize that by mentioning hard work I am eliminating a great number of people. But while I wish to encourage all, I do not wish to give false hope to those who will not work. Your achievement in golf will be directly related to what you want and how badly you want it.

It is like Norman Vincent Peale expressed in the introduction to his very popular book, *The Power of Positive Thinking.* (I paraphrase.) This book is written with a deep concern for the pain, difficulty and struggles of young players. It teaches positive thinking, positive living and positive golf. It teaches a disciplined way of life, but one which offers great joy to the person who achieves victory over himself and the difficult circumstances in the world of golf. This book is written to suggest techniques and to give examples which demonstrate that anyone need not be defeated by anything—that anyone can have peace of mind. Of this I have no doubt. In one sense there may be the "breaks" in life or in golf. But there is a spirit and method by which we can control and even determine those breaks.

The attitude of this book is direct and simple. It is written with the sole objective of helping the reader achieve his goal. I believe in certain demonstrated and effective principles which, when practiced, produce amazing results. My aim is to set them forth in a manner that the reader, feeling a sense of need, may learn a practical method by which he can build a fundamentally sound golf game. If you read this book thoroughly, absorbing its techniques, then practice the principles and formulas set forth, you can experience an amazing improvement within yourself and your game.

"Attitudes are more important than facts," according to Dr. Karl Mennenger. "Any fact facing us, however difficult, even seemingly hopeless, is not so important as our attitude toward it. How a person thinks about a fact may defeat him before he begins. We may permit a fact to overwhelm us mentally before we start to actually deal with it. On the other hand, a confident and optimistic thought pattern can modify or overcome the fact altogether."

"One of the most powerful concepts I know of is a sure cure for a lack of confidence. It is the thought that God is actually with you and helping you. Almighty God will be your companion, will stand by you, help you, and see you through. No other idea I know of is so powerful in developing self-confidence as this simple belief when practiced."–Norman Vincent Peale

I assure you that throughout this book it is my intent to positively direct the future of your golfing career by translating my method to you as though your very life depended upon your success. I have attempted to relieve any doubts you may have about how to swing the golf club. As Mr. White told me, "I'm not in a popularity contest, David. My job is to teach you how to play golf!" General Patton said, "Do I care whether the men like me? We are fighting a war. It is a killing business. I have to teach the troops how to protect themselves and to kill the enemy. I am not running for public office!"

Through my continued indulgence in this game the Scots call golf, I have found a growing need for good instruction and guidance among aspiring young golfers who are eager to learn but are often gullible and misguided. These dreams of success are easily short-lived with all the "junk" to which they are exposed. This book contains sound fundamentals and is an excellent insight into competitive golf.

Golf House, Far Hills, New Jersey

History & tradition

Royal and Ancient Club, St. Andrews, Scotland

Sir Buck, Lord of Chipping

Who is that little old white-haired man? Sir Buck, Lord of Chipping. The George Patton of Golf.

Welcome to my world. Miracles are amazing things, and as a person who believes in miracles, I cannot help but marvel every time I see one. I also classify myself as an eternal optimist, one who gets up every morning glad to be alive and thankful for God's blessings that give me hope for each day.

I would like to pass this hope and encouragement along to you by introducing you to one miracle that happened to me when I was twenty years of age.

It is hard to believe how a seemingly small and insignificant happening could have had such a dramatic effect on changing my life. Something as simple as a phone call normally would have no more lasting effect than the time it takes to hang up. Yet, it was one such phone call that even today has completely rearranged my golfing thought and made this book possible.

To this day, I can vividly remember the telephone ringing one night in the early part of June 1970, and my running into my parents bedroom to answer it. When I answered the phone, the voice on the other end was my long time friend from childhood, Doug Taylor. Through Doug I arranged with

the consent of my father, H. Allen Smith, Jr., to take a series of golf lessons from a little old white-haired man who said he didn't know much. The arrangements were made through this same white-haired man's son, Garrard. My instructor's name was Buck White, and for all practical purposes, so far as the golfing world is concerned, he might have resided at #221-B Baker Street with his wife and "partner-in-crime," Mabelle.

That was the turning point in the world of golf for me. I can honestly say that I consider Buck White to have been the foremost authority on golf and one of the greatest teachers the world of golf has ever known. Here is why. First, anyone who could spend a total of eight days with me in two years and leave me with enough knowledge and conviction to graduate from the TPD Qualifying School in the Fall of 1975 must be heaven-sent. That in itself was a miracle. You too would agree, had you witnessed a kid so far from obtaining his goal. Our first meeting lasted a total of six days in that summer of 1970 and it was not until the summer of 1972, two years later, that our acquaintance was renewed. That first summer, shortly after our first meeting, I showed immediate improvement and set both local course records in my hometown of Hattiesburg, Mississippi.

The Hattiesburg Country Club marked the beginning of golf for me. At age 12 my first round of golf, at age 14 I began working in the pro shop, at age 16 I began working on the golf course, at age 19 a Deposit Guaranty Classic contestant, at age 20 a course record 33-29=62, and at ages 39 & 40 Mid-South 4-Ball Champion.

At the Country Club I shot 62, and at the University golf course I shot 64. Those two years were like being stranded on a remote island, with no form of communication. As I was to later learn, this was my "probationary period." A pupil needs to pass through this period before graduating into basic training. Let me explain something about Mr. White and people like him. Part of his objective from the start was to weed out the "undesirable"— those who are not worthy of being students. At this stage of his life Mr. White regarded his time most valuable and he was not willing to have it wasted on the half-hearted, not to mention the pride he took in his reputation. I sensed this and it gave me the conviction to prove myself worthy. I pass along this quote from the late Tommy Armour, "I never have wasted my time on anyone who wants to play good golf, but who either hasn't any gray matter or won't use it. And I won't begin now. I prize my performance and reputation as a helpful teacher far too much to risk it on the lazy-minded." That is exactly what Mr. White was trying to get across. Aside from his great knowledge and wisdom, Mr. White's ability to evaluate and pinpoint precisely where you are on the golfing scale of one to ten, and then lay out a clear cut program for you to undertake to get you where you want to be, was his greatest asset as a teacher. Secondly, in the twelve years I knew Mr. White, I was never able to find any reason to contradict anything he has ever said. What a source of information he was! I have practiced, studied the golf swing, played with and watched the greatest golfers in the world, and in each case I have that little old white-haired man to be still batting a thousand. In most instances, I have seen how many players could have improved had they been fortunate enough to spend time with Mr. White.

One can well imagine the anxiety and uncertainty I experienced while awaiting my first meeting. My apprehension was aided by the briefing Doug and Garrard gave me as what to expect—a kind of orientation, so to speak. Mr. White, although not large in stature by any means, was preceded by a reputation that would test the "walls of Jerico! He carried with him an air of respect and authority . . . the likes of which were foreign to me in the realm of golf. Having served under General Patton in World War II, Mr White gave me the impression that this was the very General himself. Doug and Garrard were wrong . . . he was worse than had been described to me! But, in all the time I was privileged to spend with him, I can honestly say that the more direct, positive, assertive, forceful, stubborn he became, the more I responded. On numerous occasions, Mr. White said, "David, I do not pull any punches. I tell it the way it is. If you don't like it, there's the door." I do not know of any relationships, outside my family and very close friends, that I have enjoyed as much. Not only have I found all my golf instructions to be one-hundred percent sound, but I have never been able to find one error in any of our "classroom" discussions.

To this day I remember our first meeting. I had driven from Hattiesburg to the coast to meet Doug and Mr. White for a 9:00 o'clock meeting. We then drove to the Broadwater Sea Course in Biloxi. One of the first things he said was, "David, I am a very positive person." To me this meant, "David you do it my way or you don't do it at all. David, I teach 'method' . . . not manipulation."

This means that what someone else does or says does not apply here. Father once told me about a pass route he incorrectly ran in football practice at Ole Miss. As he returned to the huddle he was confronted by the coach. Daddy said, "I thought," and no sooner did he get that out than the coach exclaimed, "Don't think! Just do it the way I say." I believe this was what Mr. White was trying to convey to me. "David, I don't pull any punches; I didn't come here to babysit."

I learned in that first week that **I needed a swing that would repeat**—especially under pressure, and that **simplicity** is the ultimate objective. Mr. White called it the greatest of all attributes. Simplicity, like wisdom, is the principal thing. **The first requisite of a truly sound swing is . . . simplicity.**

We do not need complex "gimmicks," just good form. Good form in any physical activity can be valued in terms of efficiency. In golf, good form depends upon three things:

1. The development of the greatest possible clubhead speed at impact.

2. The achievement of a precisely accurate contact between clubhead and ball, directing the blow along the line which the ball is intended to travel;

3. Consistency in performing these actions.

In studying the better players it is seen that, although no two are the same, still there are certain things they all do. If I were to ask for a definition of a good swing, you might list similar characteristics of good players. Mr. White's definition of a good swing is, **"one that works."** I could tell right away this was going to be my introduction to formal golf education. I had received instructions before, mostly in my early years, as everyone should do when approaching the game of golf. But instruction and knowledge have distinct levels of ability; such as whether a teacher is capable of teaching elementary school, junior high, high school, college, or graduate school. (For me to suddenly go from high school into the likes of Armour,

Boomer, Jones, Dunn, or White was an eye opener, to say the least.)

You will know if your teacher is an accomplished instructor. This is based on the simplicity of the mechanics he is teaching you. Most teachers approach solutions by trying different means of corrections, such as "try this," "how about this," or "let's do it this way." It is a kind of "trial and error" method. Any golfer who fails to follow one set of precise instructions long enough, and without conviction, or to allow the brain to pattern consistently and exactly, is a golfer who is doomed to fail. Working with Mr. White gave me great comfort. I was finally in touch with a man who had an indepth understanding of the complexities and working knowledge of the game. He also had the wisdom and personal experience.

It is meaningless to exclude mechanics from any attempt to learn the golf swing. I would learn from reading *Golf Fundamentals* by Seymour Dunn, that the player must play it as soon as he is able, not mechanically, but through his awareness of how it should be played, as well as the "feels" which he has built around this awareness. Do not waste time questioning the use of a mechanical theory. A theory paves the way for the development of a proper sense of touch. Without a sound working theory you will not get anywhere.

"Practice by mechanical theory to form the right habits so that your swing will be correct. In playing a shot, your attention must be concentrated on what is to be done, not on how it is to be done." Seymour Dunn

Put the ball into or as near as possible to the hole. The movements involved in accomplishing these things are to be correctly performed. They are the result of properly acquired feel and touch, plowed out by repeated practice of the right kind.

If while playing a shot the mind is allowed to wander, the swing cannot be focused on the shot. Focus the conscious mind on the desired effect. This will trigger the subconscious mind to have keen control of the movements necessary to produce this effect.

Practice of mechanical theory will take you only so far. To enjoy repeated great performance, a player must learn the art of inwardly triggering for each shot the inspiration necessary to execute the shot with such skill and precision that it becomes an art form.

Iron Byron may be set to do a certain act with wonderful precision, but it cannot size up a situation and sense the extreme delicacy of touch necessary to produce that exact direction, distance and particular spin affect on the ball.

Some players play their strokes in excellent mechanical order, but they never score well and rarely experience the thrill of winning. They lack good judgement in sizing up the touch required to produce the desired effect. They lack the inspiration necessary to accomplish their goals. If you focus your thoughts on mechanical theory only it will dull your inspiration for the shot.

After acquiring the proper physical ability to produce an effective swing, acquire the habit of always triggering the inspiration necessary to accomplish the job—placing the ball in the hole. Do this on every shot.

In driving from the tee, do not drive for the fairway. You may miss it. Instead, aim your shot at a specific target, or just over the top of an imaginary directional flag which is in the

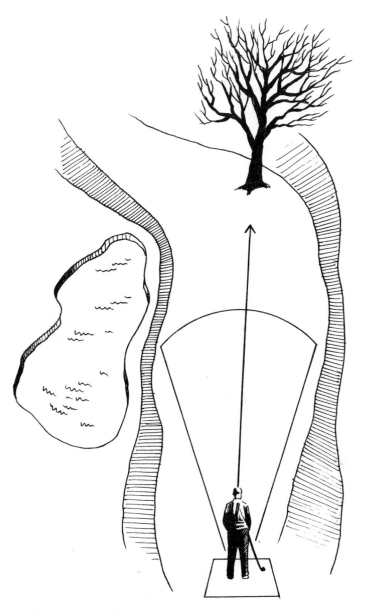

Planning your shot requires that you give your brain a direct command. When formulating your command it is best to visualize a specific target rather than a general direction.

center of the fairway. In the approach shot, do not play for the green, but play for the hole that is in the green. Take aim at it with an intense interest. Focus both mind and eye on the hole itself to get a clear impression of where it is. Inspire yourself with the thought that you are going to focus your attention on the thing to be done—put the ball in the hole.

Practice by mechanical theory to build an effective golf swing. Play by concentrating your attention on the task to be done.

Mr. White's education started from the time he was six-years-old making clubs and shaving down wooded shafts in his home town of Memphis, Tennessee. At that time wooden shafts were splinted at the end, then wrapped to the club-head.

With Memphis being the capital for persimmon clubs and hickory shafts, there was no better place to receive an education. Like most golfers of his era, Mr. White started as a caddy.

At the age of eighteen, he embarked on his professional career by signing a contract with A. G. Spalding Sporting Goods Company. His first job was at the Indianola Country Club in the heart of the Mississippi Delta. From 1929 to the early 1970's, Mr. White either worked or played as a professional golfer. The highlights of his playing career were: his tournament victories including the Memphis Open, being a member of the U.S. Ryder Cup team, and participation in numerous major tournament events including 13 U.S. Opens, 11 PGA's, 3 Masters, and 1 British open.

The nature of the times back in the 1930's, 40's and 50's, while on the pro tour, was to travel, lodge and enjoy close, meaningful relationships with other players—more so than today.

Through this constant fellowship with good players, it is easy to see how a young and inquisitive golfer would take every opportunity to learn and refine his own skills. Watching the techniques of good players proved to be an invaluable experiences.

Through countless hours of practicing, playing, and studying, Mr. White became an "authority" on golf. He was a lifetime member of the *Professional Golfers Association of America*, and until his health would not permit, he maintained a restricted teaching schedule. His dedication to the profession was exemplified by visiting tournaments whenever possible, traveling as far as the British Open, where he met golf friends, observed players, and studied swings. He told me countless times, "David, golf is my Business."

The next time you visit the Hall of Fame of Golf at Pinehurst, N.C., you will not see a bust of Buck White. If you look closely you will find one of his innovative pitching wedges. Perhaps some day the great golf teachers may be honored in like manner as the players. If so, there is no doubt in my mind, and the mind of others, who should be the first inductee. The "chairman of the board" is O'Neal "Buck" White. If Spalding honored people who had made the most contributions in clubs, it would be that same boy of eighteen to whom was given a contract back in Indianola. I hope in some way I have paid tribute to him.

When I first went to Mr. White I was a muscle-bound kid. From the beginning he made several changes that gave me peace of mind, and you know what that is worth. To have peace of mind, one must have complete faith in the instructor and confidence in the instruction he is receiving. After playing our first eighteen holes together Mr. White said, "David, when I first saw Arnold Palmer, he couldn't keep the ball on the golf course. You can't keep it in the county!" In other words, I was less than accurate off the tee. He emphasized that in order to play good golf a player needs a correct, powerful, and repeating swing—something I didn't have.

The next day on the practice tee, after I had hit a few balls, Mr. White stopped me and said, "David, let me look at your clubs. You know, David, Wilson makes a very fine club. In fact, they are so good they have taken the time to make this five iron a little longer than this seven. They also have made this five iron with less loft than the seven. In short, David, they have done such a good job that if you make the same swing with the five as you did with the seven, the ball will go further. You don't have fourteen swings just because you have fourteen clubs. I have found it a far simpler matter to change a club than a swing. Use the same swing for all clubs."

I needed a consistent, repeating swing.

By having more than one swing it is easy to understand how a person could become confused and not know when to use one or the other. Where does one stop and the other begin. One will "bleed" over into the other and hence add to the confusion. It is difficult to get confused with only one thought. Mr. White made it clear that if I changed my fundamental golf movement for the playing of any shot, that shot not only fails to help build up recallable feel and reflex movements—it actually complicates and confuses the feels and reflex movements which have been built up. You don't need several swings or mechanical options to play great golf. Great golfers became great by patterning one swing and then applying it to every shot.

The first corrections I made were:

1. Put my weight on the right side at address,

2. Take the club back by stretching my right side—turn the right shoulder back as far as I can,

3. Stretch my left side through by lifting my left shoulder up on the downswing.

You can see Mr. White believes that golf is a **two-sided** game. The purpose for stretching was not only to effectively hit good golf shots, but also to gain something I did not have;

The same centrifigal force that keeps the water from coming out of this bucket will keep the clubface true during the swing.

adding width to my swing, or "extension." I needed to stretch my muscles. The force in golf is centrifugal, like the swinging a pail of water up over and down around. The pull of the pail (club) opposes the region of the head and sternum, so the arms must be at full stretch when you come into the ball. With my physique, the bulk got in my way and often restricted my ability to turn back. The tension and strain caused by over-developed muscles is not needed in building a good golf swing. Mr. White said he considered **not getting back** to be the most common fault in swinging the golf club. I could not get back because I was too tight.

Another move I made to keep the ball from staying out to the right was to "square" the club going back on the takeaway. This was a more square position than I had been

A FOUR STEP APPROACH TO SWINGING THE CLUB
(1) Clubhead square at address,
(2) clubhead opens on the backswing with the toe of the club pointing up as the swing approaches hip level,
(3) clubhead returns sqaure up aginst the back of the ball during impact, and
(4) clubhead closes on the follow through with the toe of the club pointing up as the swing approaches hip level.

accustomed to. I did this by cupping my right hand and wrist a little on the takeaway, so that at the top of the backswing my left wrist and left hand were in a more straight line. **The clubhead still opens on the backswing and closes on**

the downswing but I had been prematurely and artificially opening the clubhead on my takeaway and I needed a little adjustment to correctly start the backswing.

Before I started this stretching motion, I always hit the ball. Like most golfers, I worked "to" the ball, not through it. By stretching my left side through, **I let the ball get in the way**, as Mr. White would say. This was the key for getting through the ball. No longer was I afraid of the ball. I do not even think of it. I just swing through it. Remember, that you cannot stretch through unless you have stretched back correctly by turning the right shoulder **all the way back.** Another point he brought out was to "plan" your shot before you swing. He was careful not to crowd my mind with more information than I could comprehend and put to use. That ended our second day.

The next day, very eager to start, I found out that from there on I would never graduate to anything over a 3/4 nine iron. Imagine how disheartening this was, because all I wanted to hit was my driver. We began the day with a sand wedge, a 1/4 sand wedge at that. This means that I could take my hands back only so far as my mid-thigh and down through the same. Because of the tremendous stretching, this was more work than I thought. Mr. White took great pride in the fact that his students woke up the next morning aching from muscles they did not know existed. With

his "hands on"approach to teaching, I was not afforded the luxury of faking it.

At this point, I was instructed to keep my weight stationary by leaving my right heel on the ground when I stretched through. How strange this was to me! Could I have been so stupid as to think the ball should have been played forward (with my weight on my left side) with a wedge to get the ball in the air? **Surely not!** I did not know that after three hours of using only 1/4 sand wedges that I would be having so much fun. Spalding prints two red stripes around their practice balls, and when struck correctly, the spin generated by a sand wedge can be exciting to see.

After a hamburger and a coke for lunch (standard operating procedure), it was back to the tee. This time it was halves and 3/4 nine irons. Mr. White's method of teaching may seem strange to you; it was to me. He would often go five, ten or fifteen minutes without saying anything. He would stand there—observing. During these silent periods, I would be tempted to ask a question or try to inject some conversation. I felt very insecure . . . like I was under a microscope. Because there was no doubt as to who was in charge, I refrained from doing so. A good rule of thumb to follow is "speak when spoken to." Mr. White had already seen more than sixty birthdays, but he had not yet acquired an appreciation for small talk. I wanted to continue my relationship with him so I felt it wise not to push the issue.

After missing shots time after time, I would finally hit one right and say, "You missed that one Mr. White, it was perfect." "Amazing," would be his reply. As if to say, see what happens when you make a good swing and let the ball get in the way. This is the routine we followed the rest of the week. In each instance, Mr. White would strongly emphasize the points he had already made. Still today, after playing poorly, I just take a very easy club like a sand wedge, pitching wedge or nine iron and swing it until I regain the right feel, knowing that if I get the right feel with these shorter clubs, I will soon be making my shots with the longer clubs correctly and with confidence.

One may say, "If this is the case, how does a player hook or slice the ball?" You just open or close the clubface at address. The idea is to be able to hit different shots without changing your method. Good golf requires that you learn to play as many of these shots as possible with the same movements. By making the necessary adjustments in the planning stage, you are free to make your normal swing without manipulating the clubhead. Bobby Locke was notorious for this. Let's say there was a tree on his right, between himself and the hole. Instead of slicing the ball from left to right he would hook the ball around it. Locke hooked everything and when it came to changing his pattern, he became increasingly stubborn.

After two years of stretching, I was ready for my second lesson. This included:

1. moving my hands at address in front of my fly or mid-thigh (left) area,

2. checking my grip before swinging, not once I was over the ball,

3. a sequence of movements on the backswing. They were:
   (a) clubhead,
   (b) hips,
   (c) shoulders.

Mr. White said, "David, you can't start the clubhead back unless your hands are in the correct position . . . up front." I did not accomplish this part of my education as well as I did the first lesson of stretching. Even today, when I feel myself slipping, I do not hesitate to go back to stretching to get back on the right track.

Mr. White refers to **going back to the basics** like a baby with a security blanket. Basics are your three P's and swing method. The basics are the fundamentals of golf. **Master the basics at all cost.** (I will explain the three "P's" in a later chapter and go over your S.O.P.)

On several occasions, Mr. White said it was a fact, and always will be so, that there is more than one way to swing a golf club effectively. He maintained that his method may not be the only way—but at least it was a way.

As students of the game of golf, we all must learn the fundamental principles, and then by diligent practice, learn to adapt them to our individuality. It is also a fact that there are no two players precisely the same—either in height, weight, strength or mentality. No one player should ever try to imitate in every detail the style of another player. Work along similar lines, but to attempt to imitate any other golfer, in every detail, would be hopeless and counter-productive. Develop your own style around your strengths. Work on the fundamental principles on which all good golfing swings are based. You will be better for it.

The next day we played at Pass Christian Golf Course on the Mississippi Gulf Coast, a course I had never played before. On the fourth hole, a par three, I asked my friend Doug Taylor, who was playing with us and also taking lessons, what he was hitting and how far did he think it was to the green.

Unknown to me was the ever present attentiveness of Mr. White. He had overheard my question and that got his dander up. "David," he said, "always get a scorecard on a new course. Do you think they are going to help you when you get on the tour?" Does Macy's tell Bloomingdale's? The answer is obvious. People are out for "blood"; if you think anyone is going to help you—you're mistaken! While everyone should play by the rules and maintain good sportsmanship, a part of athletic competition is war—especially professional sports. In America, winning is everything, whether it be business, sports, or any other endeavor.

In sports, winners are remembered and losers are forgotten. Winners have an inner drive and are willing to demand from themselves whatever it takes to win. It is this discipline that many people are not willing to endure. What would have happened if the United States had lost World War I or World War II. Too many people defeat themselves. To be a good competitor, you must want to win and hate to lose. Remember, fight until you win; never give in. Learn to look out for yourself, and don't depend on others. "There can be no defeat, if a man refuses to accept defeat. Wars are lost in the mind before they are lost on the ground."—Geroge Patton

Jimmy Connors was once quoted as saying,"You have to be a bit of a killer out here . . . not a 'bit'—you *have* to be a killer."

Later that same day we were on the ninth hole and after a good drive, I pulled an eight iron off to the left and missed the green. After hitting it I looked down at the club and instead of taking blame for the shot myself said, "This club is hooked."

Here came Mr. White again, running across the fairway, taking the club out of my hands. After examining the club, he put it back into my hands, jerked them forward and yelled, "Now how hooked is it?" I had my hands back behind the fly of my pants where they were before the previous day's lesson. This made him upset and I did not blame him. In fact, he was so upset he did not say anything for the rest of the day, including the ride home. You may think this is pretty drastic behavior on his part, but realize that young stubborn kids sometimes need to have their bell "rung" to get their attention.

In eleven years I think this was the closest Mr. White ever came to criticizing anything I ever did; and believe me, I appreciated it, because I have done some things that would have made *me* lose patience. **Teaching is best done in a positive nature. Do** this or **do** that. Good golf instruction reduces confusion by reducing the number of "do's" that the golfer is to consider during the execution of any single swing. Since there are too many "don'ts" to worry with, concentrate on the positive.

"Like I said, David," Mr. White once remarked, "I am very positive person. I don't know what you did wrong, but I know what you didn't do right."

In dealing with **do's,** your brain is able to record them and slowly train involuntary muscles to become voluntary. When you miss a shot, never think of what you did wrong. Approach the next shot thinking of what you must do right.

This point is so well taken that we would do well to consider what General Patton had to say about "training." "It is the common experience of mankind that in moments of great excitement the conscious mental process of the brain no longer operates. All actions are subconscious, the result of habits. Troops whose training and discipline depend on conscious thought become helpless cowards in battle. To send forth such men is murder. Hence, in creating an army, we must strive at the production of soldiers so trained that in the midst of battle they will still function."

This implies that the better players, or experts, are able to play golf without thinking of anything at all—except where they wants the ball to go. The fewer details that intrude upon your mind as you are swinging, the better. General Patton surmised that, "All human beings have an innate resistance to obedience, discipline removes this resistance and by constant reputation, makes obedience habitual and subconscious."

What does this have to do with golf? Everything. Your ability to discipline yourself in game conditions (sticking to your game-plan), to practice when you do not want to practice, and the obedience to stick to your first impression when making decisions, staying positive (when controlling your mental thoughts), is the difference between winning and losing. "The answer, I believe, is that the successful man carries a resourcefulness, and a quality of judgment, the lack of which dooms the other fellow, despite his mechanical skill, to a permanent place among the 'also-rans.' Knowing what to do and when to do it is the necessary complement to mechanical skill that maintains a few men at the head of the procession, with many others clutching closely, but vainly, for their coattails."—Bobby Jones

Mr. White one time said, "Do you know why Ben Hogan said he never taught anybody? It's because he never found anyone who listened." Think of that for a minute. Mr. Hogan said he could not find anyone who would *listen*. What do you think led him to believe people were such poor listeners?

When you think of the vast number of people over the years who would have given anything to have an audience with the man some call the greatest ball striker the world has ever known, you would think he would have come in contact with someone who would listen. Yet this great golfer still maintained—no one would pay attention and listen. If no one would listen to Mr. Hogan, to whom will they listen? If you are to be a good golfer, you must learn to be a good listener. Mr. White said, "What percentage of people really hear what you say, and of the percentage that do listen, how many have the time to practice? Out of those who do have time, how many will?" A teacher with something to say might take the attitude, "It's not worth my time." Mr. White was so emphatic about what he said that he had this card printed: "I know you believe you understand what you think I said. But I'm not sure you realize that what you heard is not what I meant."

To understand this statement one must study it. Remember that experts in any field are not in the habit of arguing for the sole purpose of making you understand. They do not really care if you get it or not. It is your responsibility to realize to whom you are talking. Most of us do not pay enough attention to what we are told, how we are told, or by whom we are told. Pay attention—you may learn something! No one ever learned anything while they were talking —you have to listen.

It is better to hear the rebuke of the wise, than to hear the songs of fools. (Ecclesiastes 7:5) The best golfers have the ability to tune in what is important and tune out what is not. They are selective about what they see and hear, and only take in data that is pertinent to the task at hand. When possible, surround yourself with good players and pay attention to everything; rather than take advice from any Tom, Dick, or Harry. When you are fortunate enough to find a good teacher, stay with him or her. Avoid changing from method to method, teacher to teacher. Do not be a "treasure seeker" in search of "secrets." There are not any—just practice, knowledge, and application.

But where shall wisdom be found, and where is the place of understanding? Let your search be for the truth. (Job 28:12)

"Get the truth! Get all of the facts! Sound decisions cannot be made without all of the facts!"–General Patton

Golf, for me, may one day come down to nothing but telling Buck White stories. If that day comes, I will be proud to be an authority on that Little Old White-Haired Man.

Buck Owens

Met Open 1974

Chapter 1

Course Management & Golf Psychology

You can't win without it!—The proper attitude.

"By nature, I am an eternal optimist."—Gary Player

"Discipline, which is but mental trust and confidence, is the key to all success in peace or war."—General Patton

"Never forget that golf is much more a matter of mind than muscle."—Seymour Dunn

"You are playing a human adversary; you are playing a game. You are playing Old Man Par."—Bobby Jones

Golf is a game. Play it to have fun. "Fall in love with the fun and fascination of every single shot."—Chuck Hogan

Imagine that you are playing in the Masters Tournament. It is Sunday afternoon and you are preparing to drive off the fifteenth tee. You currently enjoy a one shot lead at nine under par. As you tee up the ball a roar comes up from the direction of the green. Suddenly something tells you that you're tied. That roar could only mean that your closest competitor has just birdied. After backing off the shot to allow the crowd noise to subside, you regain your composure and prepare to play. It's all you can do to get far enough left on the tee. This gives you the best angle to play a high draw down the right side of the fairway over a series of mounds some 250 to 260 out. This also will give you the best chance, not only for a big drive, but also you are conscious of avoiding the tall pine tree down the left side that would block your approach shot to the green.

As the swing begins you feel the resistance in your right knee. Your right thigh muscles absorb the strain caused by the turning of the hips. As you stretch your way to the top of the backswing, you retain sight of the ball out of the corner of the left eye. Suddenly, and without any conscious thought, your clubhead begins its return voyage. In a fraction of a second the ball is underway. Had it not been for the momentum of the stroke your head would still be in position. But now as your right shoulder comes through, your head rotates and you pick up the ball already some one-hundred and fifty yards into its journey. What a great feeling! Well done!

You are now standing on the sixteenth tee. After throwing up a few green chippings to test the wind, you reach for your four iron. The yardage is 182 into a slight breeze. You should already guess the location of the pin. On Sunday afternoon at Augusta, you find the hole nestled just five paces over the bunker guarding the back left portion of the green. In placing our shot, we think back to 1986 when Nicklaus' remarkable tee shot returned gently down the slope that runs through the green and guards the back portion. At this time you are thankful for your pattern of play and routine, otherwise there wouldn't be any way to get this shot off effectively.

Walking to the ball, you remind yourself that this is not the time to be tentative. You must stay focused and summon the courage necessary to pull off this shot. Give yourself a big pat on the back. You did it. Nice shot. But as nice as these shots are, they don't win tournaments. It is virtually impossible to make enough good swings to come out a winner. Victory, however, as Mr. White so tactfully reminded me on more than one occasion, goes to the player who shoots the lowest score.

The object in golf is to shoot the lowest score possible.

Accomplishing that requires intelligent thought, physical effort and precise execution. Course management remains the foremost part of the game. Once the round is underway, the business at hand is that of getting the ball in the hole. Nothing else matters.

Ben Hogan once said, **"Good swings don't win tournaments—good management does."** After spending a great deal of my adult life competing in tournament golf both as a professional on the PGA Tour and as an amateur, I am entitled to agree wholeheartedly. From personal experience, I know that Mr. White spent just as long talking and trying to teach me course management as he did watching me hit balls on the practice tee. I can assure you, learning to swing a golf club is much easier.

"The secret of success in golf lies in temperament, and this is true, whatever grade of golf you may aspire to play. Tournaments are not always, not usually won by the greatest stylists. They go to the men with the best balanced outlook on the game,"—Percy Boomer

When I say that a person has a good golfing temperament I mean that he has sufficient control over his emotions to produce his best shots, whatever the circumstances may be. Any such player begins with a greater advantage over a player with ideal golfing technique or a fine natural swing.

"One thing a tournament golfer has to learn is that it is not the game he played last year, or last week, that he commands in any one event. He has only his game at the time; and it may be far from his best—but it's all he has, and he'd just as well 'harden his heart' and make the most of It."—Walter Hagen

Hagen also realized that, "the course will sometimes fail to reward all his good shots, but it will also fail to penalize all his bad ones." There are great lessons to be learned, and if you haven't, just remember that **No one was born with good management.** He had to learn just like you and me. "Mental toughness is learned, not inherited." Patton.

History has shown that great players have achieved mental toughness and consistency through acquiring a set of mental skills: such as self-motivation, positiveness, being in control of their emotions, poised in the heat of battle, self-confident, and taking responsibility for their own actions. It is important to realize that these skills are learned, not inherited. Bobby Jones said, "I never won a major championship until I learned to play golf against something, and not somebody. And that something was Par." There will be many times when things will not go your way. Do not let it get you down. It's just "the rub of the green." Remember something that any Scotsman will tell you—**golf** was never intended to be a fair game.

One day while playing on the 5th hole at the Broadwater Sea Course in Biloxi, Mississippi, Garrard White, Buck's son, hooked his tee shot a little into the left side of the fairway. As we approached we noticed that the ball had rolled up against the base of a tree. To make matters worse, not only was the tree directly between the flag and his ball, but it was the only tree within twenty yards of his ball. Neither Mr. White nor Garrard had adopted the philosophy of turning the other cheek in matters such as this, so after semi-playing the shot back out into the fairway, Garrard set forth once again to disprove the theory that spontaneous, violent eruptions and a low boiling point are not hereditary, and proceeded to personally educate a tree in the finer points on the origin of tooth picks.

I might add that Garrard continued to assault this tree verbally while walking toward his next shot. As of this writing, I can safely say that the theory is still intact. Witnessing this unfortunate incident, I remarked to Mr. White about how I thought Garrard had gotten a bad break. Mr. White, mastering all the compassion that was typical of his nature, remarked, "If he continues to play," then pausing as if to express some degree of doubt, "it will happen again." How true that is. It is your choice—play or not play.

When misfortune becomes your closest companion there is no sense in feeling victimized or cursed with bad luck. It only breeds self-pity and a losing attitude. "When you learn responsibility, you become tougher and more resilient to misfortune. You become more self-reliant and take precautions against making decisions that will hurt you."–David Graham

Since golf is an individual game, it is important that you learn to take responsibility for your own successes or failures. Every great golfer has done this. He does not make excuses and blame others for his failures. He realizes that his destiny is in his own hands, and he must rely on his faith for the strength necessary to succeed.

Perhaps no other feeling in the world is such a deterrent to discouragement and such a source of constant motivation as this feeling of destiny. What a wonderful realization it is to know that in order to accomplish His purpose for us, God has made us perfect in every way. Everything we need to succeed is not only complete, but was entrusted to us as a gift. We should all be about finding out His will for us in our lives, and diligently pursuing it–lest our gifts be taken away.

One of my favorite scenes in the motion picture "Patton" is when General Patton is facing tremendous political pressure and overwhelming odds to end his career as a military leader. The result of which would relieve him of his duty and sentencing him back to the United States before he was assigned commander of the Third Army. In the face of adversity and total discouragement, Patton drew on his inner strength to recall the single most answer to his being–his conviction of his destiny. "I feel I'm destined to achieve some great thing . . . the last great opportunity of a lifetime, an entire world at war, and I'm left out! God will not permit this to happen! I am going

to be allowed, to fulfil my destiny! . . . His will be done."–
General Patton

Believing you are destined to be something or to accomplish something is a great source of encouragement and inspiration. To Christians, destiny implies heavenly direction. We must realize our talents are gifts, and as the Bible says, "all good gifts are from above." The thought that we are carrying out Gods plan for us is the surest plan for success. So if you are not yet where you want to be, rejoice in the struggle and be thankful for the challenge. We must be very careful not to condemn our circumstances. There are two very good reasons for this: First, it may very well be that your circumstances are from above, and second, throughout history God has seen fit to inspire greatness from those with meager beginnings. Almost without exception, this has been proven in every generation .

Great entrepreneurs, great inventors, great political leaders, great military leaders, great athletics, etc. rose to greatness after having endured hardship and suffering. Look at the story of Moses in the Bible. Study the life of Abraham Lincoln. Read about Thomas Edison's failures. Think of Martin Luther King's pilgrimage. Sam Walton began with nothing until his Wal-Mart store success made him one of America's wealthiest persons. Even Warren Buffett, one of the most widely respected investors in America, went door to door raising money from his neighbors, until today his fortune is listed by Forbes to be in excess of two billion dollars. The childhood of General Stonewall Jackson was nothing to be envied: deaths in the family and constantly moving from home to home.

Sylvester Stallone's success as "Rocky," depicting his life on the streets of south Philadelphia would to this day be lost if it were not for his belief in his story and in himself. And isn't it interesting that recently his fear of failure and loss has served to motivate him to even greater heights? This highest-paid entertainer today recently said that he felt he has accomplished nothing—that each day he must prove himself over again.

One of the most successful businessmen I know, a good friend of mine, began his business career with a loan to open his first store. Ironically, the $1,100 he needed had to be secured by not one, but two banks. Today this man has been blessed many times over and is worth millions. Another friend of mine began his career as a young salesman. A multi-millionaire today, he has said that his first suit was purchased on weekly payments, and he was very concerned about meeting those weekly payments!

The greatest athlete of today, some say, is Bo Jackson. Bo grew up with no father. His mother worked more than one job to put food on the table and a roof over their heads. Recently, Bo was asked what makes him "tic." Being a family can, he said that he wanted his wife and children to have life better than he had. As a child Bo had to overcome much, but the one thing that struck terror in him (to the extent of wiping away the tears), was waiting for his mother to come home at the end of the day so he could ask her for the $5 he needed for a school field trip the next day—$5 he knew she didn't have. Bo says, as he was sweating, training, and practicing, in order that his own kids wouldn't have to have to face the other school children "without having the $5." In 1991 Bo's income was estimated at over six million.

Another man I know was born in a log cabin in rural Mississippi. His mother and father divorced early, causing him to work to help the family. Growing up with little, motivated him enough to: be awarded a college football scholarship, as a marine during World War II going through the campaign in the South Pacific, and to recover physically after sustaining three bullet wounds while leading a company of men up "Sugar Loaf Hill" on Okinawa; and under Coach George Halas to star on the grid-iron for the Chicago Bears, in the National Football League. And at the time of his death, my father had founded a successful business career as an independent oil producer.

Gary Player has been paid may compliments in his career, but the one I like most is that Gary has been called the most determined competitor. Dogmatic in nature to be the best. Could it be that the thought of working in the mines of South Africa laying on his back all day, as his father did, motivate him? I think so.

Lee Trevino constantly makes reference to his early days in Dallas. Seve Ballesteros began with only one club, sneaking on to a golf course in a little village on the north Spain. The following names began their careers in the caddie yard: Hogan, Snead, White, Rodriguez, Dent, Nelson.

Before you get the wrong impression, may I remind you, be grateful for the hardships that produce a seed of determination. Remember, your plight is the surest formula for greatness, one that the more fortunate will seldom know. Remember too, God searches out the low in spirit, the less fortunate, and the cotton fields to work his marvelous work. Truly, "AMAZING GRACE" abounds.

One of the greatest thoughts I can imagine in cases such as these is to remember a statement by the Rev. Robert Schuller: "Tough times never last, but tough people do."

Another meaningful statement that exemplifies winning more than anything is:

"No virtue in the world is so often rewarded as perseverance."—Bobby Jones

It has been said that the greatest asset of Harry Vardon was his perfect realization of the cold fact that no matter what happened once the round was underway, there was only one thing for him to do—"keep on hitting the ball."

Much of what is discussed in this chapter you may or may not know. Some things you may know but, at the same time, not be conscious of. Then again, other information may be sleep in the back of your mind. If that is the case, I will attempt to bring them up front by awaking them.

In 1970, my friend, Martha Phillips, wife of former baseball star Bubba Phillips, introduced me to a book entitled *Psycho-Cybernetics,* by Dr. Maxwell Maltz. At that time I was in the category described in the above paragraph. This book did much to enlighten me. I will summarize some of the important thoughts that will help you develop a winning attitude in your life and your golf.

The most important psychological discovery of this century is the discovery of the "self image." Whether we realize it or not, each of us carries with us a mental blueprint or pictures of ourselves. It may be vague and ill-defined to our conscious gauge. In fact, it may not be consciously recognizable at all. But it is there, complete down to the last detail.

Once an idea or a belief about ourselves goes into this picture, it becomes "true," so far as we, personally, are concerned. We do not question its validity, but proceed to act upon it as if it were true.

All your actions, feelings, and behaviors—even your abilities are consistent with your self mage. In short, you will "act like" the sort of person you conceive yourself to be. Not only this, but you literally cannot act otherwise, in spite of all your conscious intentions, or your will power, even if opportunity is literally "dumped" in your lap. The person who conceives himself to be a victim of injustice, one "who was meant to suffer" will invariably find circumstances to verify his opinions.

Good news though; the self image can be changed. "Positive thinking" cannot be used effectively as a patch or a crutch to the same old self image. In fact, it is literally impossible to really think positively about a particular situation, as long as you hold a negative concept of yourself. And, numerous experiments have shown that once the concept of self is changed, other things consistent with the new concept of self are accomplished easily and without strain.

This relieved me greatly, because I had the impression that I was inferior. I couldn't understand how a boy from Mississippi could possibly become a tour player. No one from Mississippi ever has made the tour from the new qualifying system. And to my knowledge, only Johnny Pott had ever played the tour. Not even Mike Taylor, who was "Superman" dressed up in a pair of khaki slacks and a white Izod shirt, turned pro. I thought, "Who am I, to want to be a tour player?"

I learned that the greatest obstacle between me and my goal was me.

Don't get me wrong. I think growing up in Mississippi is a great asset. But I did not know it at the time. Looking back, I think this attitude was brought about by my lack of exposure and experience in tournament play, both statewide and on a national level. Without a winning record on which to build confidence and base success it is impossible to convince yourself you are for real.

"Developing self-confidence is critical, for many other attributes follow in its wake. self-confident people are also proud, motivated, upbeat, and unafraid of success. They find it easier to summon the courage to attempt challenges others shy away from."–David Graham

I had many crazy ideas. I lacked direction, and how to find it. After reading *Psycho-Cybernetics* I thought to myself, "If I am to achieve my goal, I must change my outlook."

A few years ago I stumbled upon some of the greatest news I could imagine—almost revolutionary in nature. You are no doubt aware of the popularity of "Soap Operas." Psychologists tell us that the human nature is such that we derive a great deal of comfort from seeing other people who have the same problems and troubles as we do. Somehow, knowing we are not alone in our struggles makes us feel better about ourselves. Thus, the affection for and in some incidences, an addiction to "Soap Operas." I by no means wish to imply that I have any interest in "Soap Operas." I am emphasizing a point contained in the story from Martin Blumenson's book entitled, *Patton, the Man Behind the Legend.*

Once upon a time there was a young man who considered himself a coward. In fact, he once said, "I have always fancied myself to be a coward." So this young man seeing himself to be unfit because he lacked what he considered to be the military virtues, struggled with single minded devotion to remake himself, to alter his inner nature into his image of the fighting man. He consciously shaped the talents he had inherited, modified his strengths and outlook, stifled the qualities he regarded as unworthy, cultivated the traits he believed to be desirable, and periodically tested himself to see whether he measured up to his standards.

"Truly for so fierce a warrior," he wrote, "I have a mild expression." He started to practice before a mirror to change his countenance, to improve his fighting face. Shy and withdrawn by temperament, tending easily to tears of emotion, unsure of himself, sensitive to natural and artistic beauty, he scorned these characteristics. "A man of diffident manner," he once wrote (speaking of himself), "will never inspire confidence. A cold reserve cannot beget enthusiasm in combat. Thus, a leader must be an actor, and have fixed determination to acquire the warrior's soul. Unless he lives his part, he is unconvincing." "Underneath the rough-spoken, cold-blooded exterior," wrote a friend who knew him well, "he was a gentle and kindly person who had to make himself tough to do the job he had. **He wasn't born that way!"**

Over and over in my mind I kept wrestling with that phrase, **he wasn't born that way**. As strange as it may seem, that was the good news which, when I read it, caused me to rejoice. You see, those of us who watched George C. Scott portray General Patton in the movie *Patton* only saw the finished product. How could it be that one of America's greatest generals, a man whose life and personality caused mountains to shake and the enemy to quiver, called himself a coward? The answer is that his inner desire to fulfill his destiny caused him to remake himself into the person he had become. **He wasn't born that way.** And that was the good news, because I too considered myself a coward. And in order for me to fulfill my goals as a golfer, I am faced with the struggle to remaking myself even more today than I have done in the past.

You may think like this: I'm a bad putter, I can't play long golf courses, I can't beat, so I don't like bad weather. If you are to be a competitive golfer, you had best reconsider.

Everyone has a success mechanism put there by the Creator to aid in goal seeking.

The way to reach your goal in golf is to establish your goal first and then break it down into stages. "A goal implies desire and when you feel this desire acutely enough you will give yourself an atomic power that will help propel yourself toward the opportunities that the day brings. You insist on fulfilling yourself, you will not take no for an answer."—Maxwell Maltz

Be realistic. Don't fool yourself; face facts. **No one becomes the greatest golfer overnight.** Be patient—and have little goals along the way. Never get discouraged; everyone has his ups and downs. Mr. White has reinforced my self-steem after bad judgments and mistakes, many times saying, "I haven't met a man yet who doesn't make mistakes." I think to myself, "What a wonderful way to teach, rather than to criticize." Bobby Jones said, **"I never learned anything from a match that I won; I got my golfing education from drubbings."** So remember, "only the strong survive." The way to evolve as a golfer is always to believe in yourself and believe you are improving and try to improve. You always have to project to yourself a positive image of your game. This is good advice.

Listen to what General Patton wrote to his son. **"Self-confidence is the surest way of obtaining what you want.**

If you know in your own heart you are going to be something, you will be it. Do not permit your mind to think otherwise. It is fatal." My observations lead me to believe that every champion has a deep, unwavering belief in himself as a person and his ability to play well. These performances are born from building self-confidence. Self-confident people are indestructible and are unaffected by what others say or do. "Supremely self-confident people are resilient to setbacks, welcome pressure, and are not easily defeated."–David Graham

Mr. White would send me on my way many times with these parting few words of instruction; "David, do one thing for me–think of being positive."

Getting back to *Psycho-Cybernetics,* a human being always acts and feels to perform in accordance with what he imagines to be true about himself and his environment. You act and feel, not according to that things are really like, but according to the images your mind holds of what they are like. Picture yourself vividly as winning and that alone will contribute immeasurably to success. Great living starts with a picture, held in your imagination, of what you would like to do or be. Your present self-image was built upon imagination; pictures of yourself in the past which grew out of interpretation and evaluation which you based upon experience.

Remember that your automatic mechanism can as easily function as a *failure mechanism* as a *success mechanism,* depending upon the data you give it to process and the goals you set for it.

It is basically a goal-striving mechanism. The goals it works upon are up to you. Many of us unconsciously and unwittingly set up goals for failure by our attitude and imagination.

Also remember that your automatic mechanism does not reason about nor question the data you feed it. It merely processes it and reacts appropriately to it.

It is very important that the automatic mechanism be given true facts concerning the environment. This is the job of conscious rational thought: to know the truth, to form correct evaluations, estimations and opinions.

In *As a Man Thinketh* we find these words: "Having conceived of his purpose, a man should mentally mark out a straight pathway to his achievement, looking neither to the right not the left. Doubts and fears should be rigorously excluded. They are disintegrating elements which break up the straight line of effort, rendering it crooked, ineffectual, useless. Thoughts of doubt and fear never accomplish anything and never can. They always lead to failure. Purpose, energy, power to do, and all strong thoughts cease when doubt and fear creep in."

A definite sense of purpose also adds a strong motivation toward making the most of your abilities. We all know that purpose makes the difference; a clear picture of what we wish to accomplish and the determination to reach our goals strengthens our power to achieve it.

I can remember Mr. White saying, "David, for goodness sake, walk down the fairway and forget about everything else." Before you say it, let me beat you to it. How can one person be so negative? I must have tried his soul. To have been given a father of mystical strength and purpose, and a teacher so positive that old "blood and guts" would have been proud of him—my cowardice must have been a great disappointment to others, and will be until it is changed. You know, God doesn't hate cowards—He hates cowardice.

General Patton said, "Anyone who enters battle and says he's not scared is either a moron or a liar. The time to take counsel of your fears is before you make an important battle decision. When you have collected all of the facts and fears made your decision, turn off all of your fears and go ahead!" The successful golfer takes his time sizing up his shot and when he has done this he goes right up and hits the ball.

Everyone gets scared. Being scared and nervous is part of the game and a successful competitor learns to control and use his emotions to his advantage. "Faith and confidence builds pride, and pride destroys fear."—General Patton

Many times I have been nervous either because of doubt and fear or maybe because I was scared I would miss. Maybe even afraid of succeeding? "Any man who is afraid of failure will never win."—General Patton Without confidence there can be no correct poise. Without poise there can be no good results.

Mr. White said, "For goodness sake David, don't be afraid; after all, **what takes place—the trouble (course) or the swing?** Don't think about the negative, only your ability. Trust your swing. **Make the best swing you can (which is the only swing you have control over), and go from there."**

I carry this verse of scripture in my wallet. It has helped on many occasions: *Be strong and of a good courage; be not afraid, neither be thou dismayed; for the Lord thy God is with thee whithersoever thou goest.* (Joshua 1:9)

With the competition today, a golfer must have desire and an unbending determination. Jack Nicklaus was once asked what quality separated the great from the good; winners from losers. "Without a doubt," he said, "I would choose determination." All top competitors know that success requires a spirit of determination to approach every situation with enthusiasm and optimism. **"Some people call it luck, some genius; I call it determination."**

"Great people are ordinary people with extraordinary amounts of determination."—Patton

Determined individuals are hard to beat.

Through desire a man, having separated himself, seeketh and intermeddleth with all wisdom. (Prov. 18:1)

Someone once said, "The largest part of success is the will to be successful." How true this is. You must think you can.

THINK

If you think you are beaten, you are;
If you think you dare-not, you don't:
If you like to win, but think you can't
It's almost a cinch you won't.

If you think you'll lose, you're lost.
Far out in the world we find
Success begins with a fellow's will
It's all in the state of mind.

If you think you're outclassed, you are;
You've got think high to rise.

You've got to be sure of yourself
Before you can win the prize.

Life's battles don't always go
To the strongest or faster man,
But sooner or later the man who wins
Is the one who Thinks He Can.

Author Unknown

As I was growing up I very often did not play my best. Not realizing this would be a pattern for many years to come, I would deceive myself by thinking; that's alright because I can do better, or I missed three short putts, or I would have won if I had not had a hurt back, or I never played the course before. In short, when things did not go my way, I would find something to justify my not putting forth my best effort, or maybe even quitting. However, this is not the way to play the game nor is it the correct attitude.

Golf tournaments do not come along when you and your swing are ready for them. You have to take them when they come and do the best you can. I even got to the point where I would never try my best unless I got off to a good start and everything went my way. Think for a second how many rounds you have played when everything has gone your way—I must have quit on virtually every round. I would dare say that if you continue to play, you could go the rest of your life without a perfect round. And it seems that those were the only ones I was interested in playing. I wish someone would have observed me or could have looked inside my head and shown me the effect this would have on me later in life.

In short, these excuses will never profit anyone. Again, let me bring out a point I hope will be one of the themes of this book. That is the ability of evaluating correctly where you are on a scale of one to ten. Have you ever had someone ask you instructions on how to get somewhere? Especially over the phone? There are two important things you need to know. First, where are you, and second, where do you want to go. Apply this to your golf game. Where are you and where do you want to go?

Remember, be truthful and don't deceive yourself. You are what you are, nothing more, nothing less. Your ability must be substantiated by either scores or records. You are what you shoot—It doesn't matter if you missed three 1/foot putts for a score of 78 instead of a 75, as far as the world of golf is concerned you are a 78 shooter. Especially Mr. Beman and Mr. Tuthill. You just need to work on your putting.

If you are a good player and have a bad round, do not disregard your poor score as I would do and make excuses. Realize it for what it is—a bad round, but as good or bad as it may be it's yours, and it is the only measure by which we determine who wins and who loses. Your good or bad round is current—not yesterdays and surely not tomorrow. Today is the only day that counts. I have seen and heard too many people say someone has great potential. While potential is wonderful, it just as often causes a distorted view of one's self. The next thing you know those same people who praised you will say, "There goes so and so. He never lived up to his potential."

I do not know the exact reason, but I've struggled with becoming a "competitor" in golf, or in any other environment that is not very familiar to me. Because of my inadequacies in this area I have often marveled at those athletes who's strongest characteristics is their "competitiveness." My good friend,

Bob Cornett, is as efficient as anyone swinging the club, but to me this is overshadowed by the fact that Bob is the epitome of a competitor. So much so his nickname is "Scrap-Iron." I suggest you thoroughly search out the lockeroom for other possible bets before tackling the Bob Cornett's of this world. Another friend of mine, Jack Slocum, is so tough that it caused my trusted friend, Gary Cooper, to remark, that Jack could swim ashore from the Titanic. Truly, there are some people you just don't want on your heels.

We have already paid tribute to the Gary Player's and the Jimmy Connor's of this world, but I can't help but mention one of the best examples of this competitive characteristic which is clearly expressed in the career of Wayne Levi. In my observation Wayne has been in contention to win on the PGA tour maybe 15 times or so. With his four wins in 1990 I believe that brings his total to something like eleven or twelve wins. That is amazing to me. What a fierce competitor.

I am showing signs of improvement lately, having won the Florida State Mid-Amateur Championship in 1986 and the Florida State Amateur Stroke Play Championship in 1987 and the Match Play Championship in 1988. I must admit, in all other sports played, I thought I was the best and no one could beat me. I was determined to win the race and I did. One of the best compliments you will ever receive is for someone to call you good "competitor."

If there is one characteristic that will equalize someone of lesser ability to someone of greater, it is this characteristic of competitiveness.

Competitors love to compete. They love to win and hate to lose. The very thought of losing is hateful to a real competitor.

If you are to evolve as a tournament golfer, I suggest you acquire some of this competitiveness.

Later in my relationship with Mr. White this aspect of my golf was uncovered after carefully reviewing my actions. He said, "David, you are **quitting,** and that is a very bad habit to get into." Well, that is precisely what it was, a habit, and habits are hard to break. **Don't quit during a round, play it out!** Do not quit mentally and do not quit physically and pick up. Play the round out as hard as you can and if it is earthly possible—turn an 80 into a 79. In fact, I putt with a "Burke save-a-shot" putter. And every time I pull it out of my bag I am reminded of the importance of saving every shot possible. Salvage every shot you can; no matter what, do not give up! You cannot imagine the effect this will have on our future . . . either positive or negative. Let me implore you to make yourself a **vow**. Now, repeat after me:

I will never quit during a round. I will never pick up. I will play every shot to be best of my ability, one at time, so long as I live, amen.

Remember, you have made a vow to yourself and to your conscience. In one of his famous speeches to the people of Britain during World War II, Sir Winston Churchill told the people that there were three things they must do:

1. Never quit;
2. Never, never quit;
3. Never, never, never quit!

As we journey through life we should make a habit of keeping our eyes and ears open. Some wisdom and experience can only be learned over time. Many things totally unassociated with golf can add lasting value to your game. One such case has benefited me time and time again. Years ago I was listening to Chicago Bear Hall of Fame running back, Walter Payton, describe his theory on running the football. Walter was born in Columbia, Mississsippi and attended Jackson State University.

His football coach im-pressed on Walter that it was inevitable that he would eventually be tackled, but that he should do his best to pre-vent the tackle or at least delay being tackled as long as possible. He in-stilled in Walter the fact that he didn't have to take the blow. Instead, he could deliver the blow. This stayed with  Walter all through his career. Walter said his philosophy on running was to go down fighting—to "die hard."

In golf it is also inevitable that good shots will follow bad. There will be good days and bad. The more you play the more you will experience both. Sometime ago I applied Wal-ter Payton's philosophy on running to my game. After experi-menting with it in many situations I finally found the greatest benefit for me. I decided that if I was going to make a bogie, I was going down fighting. Now in my mind as I stand over a difficult putt for par I say to myself, "die hard."

DON'T QUIT

When things go wrong, as they sometimes will,
When the road you're trudging seems all up hill,
When the funds are low and debts are high,
And you want to smile, but you have to sigh,
When care is pressing you down a bit,
Rest, if you must—but don't you quit.

Life is queer with its twists and turns,
As everyone of us sometimes learns,
And many a failure turns about
When he might have won had he stuck it out
Don't give up though the pace seems slow
You might succeed another blow.

Often the goal is nearer than
It seems to a faint and faltering man,
Often the struggler has given up
When he might have captured the victor's cup.
An, he earned too late, when the night slipped down,
How close he was to the golden crown.

Success is failure turned inside out
The silver tint of the clouds of doubt
And you never can tell how close you are,
It may be near when it seems a far;
So stick to the fight when you're hardest hit
It's when things seem worst that you mustn't quit.

Author Unknown

There have been many times when I would have profited from the lesson to be learned from this poem. I can remember there have been times when once I decided I could not win the tournament, I would quit, and wind up back in the pack. In the 1977 Long Island Open played that year at the Meadowbrook Country Club I made this cardinal mistake. After a bad hole and falling a few shots behind the leader, I quit. I do not mean I picked up; I quit mentally and went through the motions on the remaining holes, finishing the tournament in 6th place. At times like this that a little bell should go off in our heads to remind us that:

Patience resides on the side of winners.

Our opponent is **"Old Man Par."** After all, Old Man Par is the toughest opponent you can face, but if you play him and play him well, you will be amazed at the outcome.

Upon reviewing my performance over the phone with Mr. White, I heard him say, "David, if you can't finish first; then for goodness sake, finish second! But better late than never; so let's get with it." Remember you **"can't look back,"** as told to me by that same Mr. White.

In essence, this whole chapter may be summarized with one word, "attitude." One's mental outlook on the way he views life, sees himself, and approaches the game of golf is the single greatest factor in determining success or failure.

As a child, I could tell my parents had studied the Bible thoroughly. One part in particular, my father had down pat. The part about "not sparing the rod" he had especially memorized. Although I was on the receiving end of many whippings the large majority of them came under the heading of "attitude adjustment." For some reason I was deficient in areas my father thought pertinent to building character and developing the proper work ethic.

If I were handing out demerits for improper attitude on a golf course, my good friend Gary Cooper would win hands down. I can remember many years ago when my wife, Bert, and I were first married. She had saved up her True Value stamps. These stamps were placed into books which she occasionally redeemed for desired items. On one of my birthdays Bert gave me a hammer for which she had saved stamps. It seemed like a lot of books.

I know that if the same system were set up for handing out demerits on a golf course, Gary could redeem his books for a Sony Trinitron and matching VCR. When it comes to "moping." Gary has won five "Oscars" The performances are something to behold. And the amazing thing is that it takes so little to set him off. He literally thrives on misfortune, bad luck, playing conditions, etc. Even Orson Wells, who once evacuated New York City during a rendition of *The Day the Earth Stood Still,* could not lend any more credibility to Gary's audio dissertations.

Gary's single criteria for determining great golf course architecture is that the ninth green and the tenth tee be separated by one common denominator; a parking lot. Gary maintains he reserves the right to "car key it" at the end of nine holes. Many times when I have been standing over a putt on the ninth green to go up say, 3 and 1, I could detect the slight clattering of car keys in Gary's pocket. I can't tell you how many putts I've missed during this psychological warfare, just to keep him going to the back nine.

Although witnessing this is quite humorous during a $2.00 nassau or among a friendly foursome, the aspiring competitor must avoid such symptoms as though they were the plague. The first-class golfer should aspire to greatness, both physically and mentally.

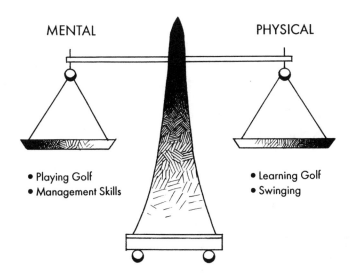

People often make the mistake of living in the past. They often refer to "what might have been" or to the "good old days." I am here to tell you that the good old days are now. **You must live in the now—today.** Not tomorrow, because tomorrow may never come. This reminds me of what I almost regard as an old Negro spiritual. I recall what an old black man said in response to a friendly greeting by another passerby. You never know where wisdom is going to raise its head. I visualize this Uncle Remus like character, who, like Old Man River, had seen many seasons come and go. From underneath his hoary head came the reply, *"Life—sho be daily."* (I make it a point to say this statment to myself each day.) You cannot be under the impression that "it" does not matter that I am a little *off* now because when the tournament comes next week, I will have it. Some who take this attitude stay "a week away." Others say, when I become a professional, I will really work. Now is the time to "really work." Recalling the past only to assist in making corrections and improvements. Strive to improve by moving ahead.

AHEAD

Those who win are those who try;
Not the kind who alibi!
Start, and never let it die
Keep moving!

Life will never bring success
To the man who's motionless;
Crowns are made for those who press
Keep moving!

Do you want to gain the prize?
All those castless realize?
There's no limit but the skies
Keep climbing!

Those who've won are round about
When you score you'll hear them shout!
Let no foe your courage flout
Keep fighting!

Sure! It's worth it when you stand
With that chosen, faithful band
Who inherit Canaan Land
Keep striving!

Guess there won't be much to do
When you're dead, and buried too:
Now's the time to see it through
Keep driving!

On to vict'ry! Never quit!
Heroes make a drive for it!
Here's Life! Use it every bit
Keep living!

Author Unknown

This poem enforces many of the points I have tried to bring out. Living and working in the now is very sound advice. *Whatsoever thy hand findeth to do, do it with all thy might; for there is no work, nor device, nor knowledge, or wisdom, in the grave, whither thou goest.* (Ecclesiates. 9:10)

"I do not fear failure. I only fear the slowing up of the engine inside of me which is pounding, saying, keep going, someone must be on the top, why not you?"—General Patton

Mr. White described the next point of course management in this way; "David, you're not playing **shot-for-shot.**" After reviewing many of my notes and my records of play, Mr. White came to the conclusion that in my thinking I often got ahead of myself or I let the last shot I played disturb my next one.He said the only shot that matters is the one you are playing. Bobby Jones said, "All of us, from duffers to champions, would be better if we would play each stroke as a thing to itself." Aside from determination, I consider this the single greatest quality in course management.

Many other great golfers have learned this lesson. Walter Hagen not only recognized that good rounds would eventually follow bad, he also learned early in his golfing life the invaluable lesson that bad shots are part of the game. He observed that they are best forgotten. The only shot that really matters is the one coming up. Bobby Locke said he learned three things early:

1. Physical relaxation or at least lack of muscular tension is essential to playing good golf shots.
2. The game can only be played one shot at a time.
3. There will always be an element of luck in golf.

However you term this, playing "shot-for-shot" is a must for tournament golf.

Two other things I would like to confront you with are:

1. It is the job of your conscious mind to pay strict attention to the "task at hand."
2. Our creative mechanism cannot function or work tomorrow. It can only function in the present.

Each of us, regardless of our achievements in golf, has to pay attention to the job at hand. Playing shot-for-shot means exactly that. Do not think about a past shot, or some future only this one. In a qualifying round for the 1976 Jacksonville Open, I needed to make a six foot putt on a hard par three. Because I had an easy par five coming, I did not give this one my full concentration. I missed the par three putt, did not birdie the par five as I had anticipated, and missed qualifying by one shot. I did not have my mind on the putt. I was not playing **shot-for-shot.**

Next in course management is **"staying to yourself."** You learn to harden your heart to everyone and everything about you so that you can concentrate on yourself, not others. Gene Sarazen said, "Your game counts for you and mine for me." Mr. White told me just before I went on the tour, "David, I have got one thing to say to you; get you a pair of earplugs" He was right. Do not listen to anybody. They want to mess you up. Once you get your "game plan" down, do not change it. Evaluate what you can do, not others.

Jack Nicklaus was playing with Gary Player in England. When they came up to a par three. Requiring they play into the wind, Gary hit first, using a seven iron. Jack, thought to himself: "I normally hit the same club or one less, so I will hit a seven too." He put his six iron back. To make a long story short, Jack came up short. This is the lesson. Many factors contribute to how far you hit with a certain club, such as;

1. How much loft does the club have?
2. How long it is?
3. Did you hook or slice the ball?
4. Where did you play the ball in your stance?

In essence, know your own game and stick to it.

Finally—do your best on very shot. Give **"total"** as Mr. White says. Having the pride and optimism to give it your best in difficult situations makes it that much easier to succeed, regardless of the cumstances. When you walk off the course you should be able to say, "I tried my best. I gave every shot my **all.**" When you can say that, you're on your way to success.

"Doing one's best, whatever the results, is winning," said General Patton's father.

Chapter **2**

The Grip

Your Only Link With the Club

The first skill that a beginner should learn is the grip, or how to hold the club. Good golf begins with the grip. Most people overlook this part because they do not understand its importance. The grip has to be good because a player's only contact with the club is through his hands. To me, the grip is a dead giveaway of a person's knowledge of the game of golf and often his ability to play. (I have always admired the way Mr. White and Mike Taylor place their hands on the club.)

With a poor grip, you are looking for trouble right away. It will affect your set-up, your takeaway, your ability to manage the club at the top, and in turn your success at striking the ball. In order to achieve success, a golfer needs to know that he must maintain a fixed relationship throughout the swing between his hands and the face of the club. Don't underestimate the way you hold the club. My grip has undergone many changes as I have learned more about golf. Don't worry if you cannot get it at first; most do not. Today, the standard grip is the overlapping grip. There are two others—the interlocking and the ten-finger grip. The overlapping was perfected by Harry Vardon about a century ago, around the late 1890's.

In a good grip both hands work as a unit. In the overlapping grip the little finger of the right hand overlaps the forefinger of the left. The first step is to place the left hand on the club so that the back of your hand is facing the target. The shaft sits under the muscular pad at the inside heel of the palm, and the shaft runs diagonally across to the top joint of the forefinger. Next, hook the forefinger around the shaft. Now, close the hand with the rest of the fingers. The thumb runs down the top of the shaft or slightly to the right. When you have completed the left hand grip, the V formed between the thumb and forefinger will point toward the right side of your head. When completed, the main pressure points are the last three fingers. While these keep pressure on the shaft, the palm pad pressure does three things:

1. strengthens the left arm throughout the swing,
2. prevents the club from slipping out of your grasp at the top of the backswing,
3. acts as a firm reinforcement at time of impact.

Too tight a grip will immobilize your wrist; so don't over-do it. The most common fault among poor golfers is that their grip is too much in the palms. This restricts the wrist from hinging properly. Place the club in the right hand so that the shaft lies across the top joint of the four fingers and directly below the palm. The two middle fingers supply the major part of the pressure. Now, with your left hand on the club, overlap the little finger of your right hand with the forefinger of the left. Then bring your right thumb down on the shaft, just slightly to the left. The knuckle of your right forefinger, directly above the shaft, should exert pressure inward toward the thumb. This should form a good V. This V points toward the right side of your face and runs parallel to the V of your left hand. The proper right hand grip will enable the greatest amount of controlled clubhead speed. This will deliver a square clubface to the target at impact. For the most power the fingers should be touching each other, not spread wide apart.

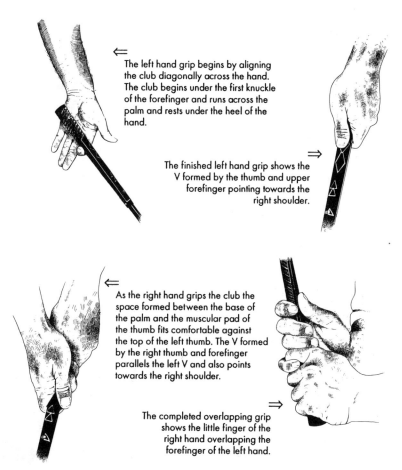

⇐ The left hand grip begins by aligning the club diagonally across the hand. The club begins under the first knuckle of the forefinger and runs across the palm and rests under the heel of the hand.

⇒ The finished left hand grip shows the V formed by the thumb and upper forefinger pointing towards the right shoulder.

⇐ As the right hand grips the club the space formed between the base of the palm and the muscular pad of the thumb fits comfortable against the top of the left thumb. The V formed by the right thumb and forefinger parallels the left V and also points towards the right shoulder.

⇒ The completed overlapping grip shows the little finger of the right hand overlapping the forefinger of the left hand.

Chapter 3

The Three "P'S"

PLANNING
PATTERN
POSITION

"It is not solely the capacity to make great shots that makes champions, but the essential quality of making very few bad shots."–Tommy Armour

PLANNING

Planning is the first of the three "P's." Never hit a shot, even in practice, without having an in-focus picture of the shot in your mind. The mind acts as a computer and your body works off the data that is stored in your brain. You program your mental computer by visualization, imagination, and other mental thoughts. Always stay in the positive. When you have decided the shot you want to hit, visualize how such a swing feels, or perhaps take a practice swing. Before you play a shot you should have already made up your mind how it ought to feel. Your control lies in your ability to remember the feeling. I also take the swing in my mind. I am retrieving an image of that swing from the memory in my computer, the subconscious; and doing it through evoking the right mental image. The mental image retrieved is as complete as I can make it: the swing itself, how it feels hitting the ball, how the ball flies, lands, and runs up to the hole. I see the ball from the moment it leaves the club. I see its trajectory, the bounce, the roll—everything.

How do the muscles of the body receive their instruction? Their initiative is born from the mind and the mind gets its inspiration through the eye. Therefore, in aiming, do not just glance at the spot you want to hit; also look at the ball, the hole or direction flag—so that the eye will register clearly on the mind what is to be accomplished. Then, the mind can properly instruct the muscles to perform the proper action. Continue to look until the eye focuses clearly on the objective. Then the eye will register on the mind the exact distance and direction of the hole or direction pole. By setting a definite target for every shot you commit your brain to an objective. With proper programming, you get the right readout and you are on your way to progress. There is no time for the negative to creep in. Remember that every shot must have a finite, predetermined target.

I am not one who continually rehearses his mistakes. When you hit a bad shot, make it a rule not to be too hard on yourself. I try to recognize mistakes, learn from them, and not make them again. Accentuate the good things. Stay in the positive. Never criticize the course or the elements. Doing so will make room for negative thoughts. Remain positive, even though things may not be going your way. Be patient. The more you play, the more positive qualities you will have. This is part of the game.

Good golfers are good planners. Your plan is for you and no one else. Once you have planned your shot or a game plan, stick with it. Always play the percentages, never **gamble.**

Scramble—don't gamble

"The greatest improvement in my game in the last five years has been a growing disposition for calculating a different situation, and an increasing distaste for the taking of reckless chances."–Bobby Jones

I have taken the risk of gambling too many times, only to discover the odds were stacked against me. There is nothing worse than walking off the course after the last hole and saying to yourself, I wish I hadn't gambled back on hole so and so. I didn't know things would turn out as they did.

"The secret of success is being consistently accurate in play, rather than occasionally brilliant. Be methodical and systematic, both in your choice of implements and in your manner of using them. Have a theory by which to work in solitary practice, and by practicing the proper theory, become naturally correct. Then when you go to play a match game, leave theory in your locker and play natually."–Seymour Dunn

The next time you think you have to gamble, consider this quote from the book, *Psycho-Cybernetics*: **"Men are disturbed, not by things that happen but by their opinion of things that happen."**

What could happen or will happen is merely an opinion, not a fact.

Those golf fans who were fortunate enough to have tickets to the *Masters* in 1987, or watched it on television, witnessed a heart-touching experience as Seve Ballesteros and his brother, after Seve's elimination in the playoff, dejectedly walked back up the tenth fairway. In a moment of utmost importance, this tremendous champion fell prey to exactly what we are talking about. He made a decision on an opinion, rather than fact.

The playoff included Greg Norman, Larry Mize and Seve. Seve's well-played iron shot struck the green, but released just behind and above the hole, into the first cut of grass. Larry hit a brilliant approach shot just under the hole and had what looked to be a very makeable birdie putt. At this point you would have been hard-pressed to find anyone, including Seve and Greg, who thought Larry would not make three. For those of us who have never been in this position, it is easy to "Monday-morning quarterback." But the fact remains that Seve's putt back down the hill and bending sharply to the right was a putt that needed to be treated with the utmost respect. Trying to make the putt, Seve rolled it by a considerabe distance and then missed it coming back for a three-putt—bogie-five. Greg parred and the world awaited Larry's attempt. He missed.

Larry was able to hole a remarkable chip shot on the eleventh green to win the Masters, but Seve was not there to see it. As the crowd noise mushroomed through the trees and up the tenth fairway back to the clubhouse, reaching Seve's ears, I am sure he reflected on his disgust and disappointment. Perhaps, had he made his decision on fact, and not opinion, his attempt on the first putt would have been one of greater percentage—a more cautious putt.

This is why we should reinforce good principals daily. While this great champion had made thousands of right decisions before; this day he proved himself human. Hopefully, we can learn from his miscalculation and sudden loss.

If you were situated at the thirteenth hole during the 1982 Masters tournament, or watching it on TV, you would have seen this incident. On Sunday afternoon, within the span of one hour, and in the last few groups, virtually everyone who was in contention, including the leader Craig Stadler, saw his second shot go into the creek. If these people, who represent the world's greatest golfers, "go in the water," think what lesser golfers have to look forward to. Don't get me wrong. I love aggressive play and I highly recommend it. What I am saying is, calculate the odds and plan effectively. Play the shot you've got the greatest chance of playing well, and play the shot that makes the next shot easy. Even the bold and aggressive are limited to what they can do.

Good course management requires the skills of a composer. Just as one note flows into another, one golf shot should flow into the next. Not all strokes require maximum force—some hard—some not so hard. You will find that good scoring requires good composition.

"We must always know exactly what we know and what we do not know—and never get the two confused. Wars are won by knowing exactly what we know."–General Patton

Because someone has the lead in a tournament doesn't mean he will win. Other competitors also have troubles. You do not have to play every round, or even one round of a tournament perfect to win. Put several good rounds together, and you too, can be a winner. The strain of tournament play wears on every participant. That one lost stroke does not necessarily have to be reconciled at once. All is not lost. Other players may also be losing a stroke. "After all, it's **Old Man Par** and you, match or medal. And Old Man Par is a patient soul, who never shoots a birdie, and never incurs a bogie. He's a patient soul, Old Man Par. And if you would travel the long route with him, you must be patient, too."—Bobby Jones

Many a person has faltered and given up leads they could have won had they stuck to the task when adversity hit. Make your judgement on **facts** not **opinions.**

Your planning should include the following:

1. type of shot you're to play,
2. what club,
3. where you want to hit the ball,
4. whether to go for it (if the odds are in your favor) or lay up,
5. weather conditions,
6. how you're going to swing the club,
7. what type of swing (whether it be full or 1/2, etc.),
8. ball position,
9. your routine or set-up position.

Mr. White maintained that during the execution of a shot he would not think of any details. I find this to be entirely true with my own play. I do all my thinking as I prepare to play. Once the swing is underway, the only thing I can think of is hitting the ball according to my programmed plan. If I attempt to think of anything else or try to make any corrections I am courting absolute ruin. I advocate making a practice swing before walking to the ball. It need not be the actual swing you make over the ball, but it should include any program keys you have at the time. This practice swing will serve to loosen you up and give you something to simulate over the ball.

Finally, your "plan" should be complete before you move the ball. **Never plan over the ball.** This is not the time to worry about the correctness of your plan. A good golfer steps up to the ball knowing exactly how he is going to hit the shot. He makes his plan in advance. See how closely this parallels the stratagy of one of the greatest tactitioners of all times. "After you make a decision, do it (with all your might) - and never take counsel of your fears over whether you made the right decision or not."–General Patton

PATTERN

Watch a great player hit a few shots during a competitive round. See that he has set a "pattern" of actions from the time he arrives at the ball to the time he begins his swing. Through this pattern of actions his ability as a player is demonstrated before he swings the club. His outine contributes as much to the success of his game as any style he may embark on the ball. Under extreme pressure this machine-like pattern doesn't change. This pattern of actions serves two practical purposes: It induces the right movements and eliminates faulty ones. It is through his routine that a good golfer senses his movements before he swings.

Your routine is a continuous gathering of power. Each feel in the whole movement is joined together with the one to follow—anticipating it, so to speak. By this I am suggesting that the feel precedes the movement. You must prepare your feel for the shot as you walk to the tee, as you are over the ball, and on through the waggle. You are continuously anticipating. You recall the correct feels and their correct succession, and you step up to the ball conscious and confident of what will happen. There is nothing to interrupt your swing—no hesitation and no hurry; the anticipation has established the correct continuous feels in them before you start.

Go through the routine, regardless of the shot or putt. Bobby Jones said, "I felt most comfortable and played better golf when the entire movement was continuous. Whenever I hesitated or took a second waggle, I could look for trouble." A pattern forces me to be deliberate, but not too much, and allows me time to calculate and process the elements of the shot I'm about to play. It insures that my mind remains focused on the key fundamentals: such as alignment of the clubface and the body, the distance I stand away from the ball, and correct positioning of the ball. It gives me a positive nature—eliminating the negative. I have no time to think where the ball could go, because I am constantly thinking of where I want it to go. A good routine sets your body in motion—which triggers the coming sequence. It focuses your mind on executing the shot; not on the consequences of a faulty execution.

Whenever I deviate from my pattern, I open the door to the negative, and ruin my rhythm and timing. Establishing a repetitive, rhythmic, systematic procedure of approaching the ball and positioning yourself confirms trust and confidence in your swing. Jones said, "Having decided upon the club to use and the shot to be played, I could see no reason for taking any more time in the address than was necessary. The more I 'fiddled' around arranging the position, the more I was beset by doubts which produced tensions and strain." How true this is. As soon as Mr. White brought my attention to this I had more success. I have spent lots of time (though not enough) walking to the ball, positioning myself, and swinging in the least possible time. The purpose was to get the shot off quicker than I was accustomed. Oftentimes, in order to speed up I say, "Do this, do that, and go." Accenting the positive and eliminating the negative is the key.

The purpose of your pattern is two-fold:

1. to insure that each time you consistently do the same things,
2. to eliminate the negative.

After losing my tour card, in the spring of '78, I tried to regain it by going back through the TPD Qualifying School. I was successful in the regional qualifying in Florida, and was on my way to the finals held at the New Mexico State University Golf Course in Albuquerque. After two practice rounds, I called Mr. White to check in and go over my previous rounds. The following is my recollection of our phone conversation:

I began by saying how hard the course was and how high the rough areas. With a tone of doubt in my voice, I also expressed how well I would have to play to make it. You should have heard what came over the phone from the other side. You'd have thought Coach Lombardi was speaking.

"David," his voice quivering, "do they have a fairway?"

"Yes," I replied.

"Then, would you put the ball on the fairway and forget everything else? You're not thinking positive if your thinking about the rough. David, all you can do is walk to the ball with your hands up front, play one shot at a time, make the best swing you know how to make, and go from there. After all, David, if you don't think you can play good you shouldn't be there. Nobody is making you play. Consider the alternative— you can come home."

Then he hung up.

I opened with 71, then 72, and had I not made the mistake of hitting a drive out of the fairway in the last round I would have regained my card. I must have thought there was some rule that said you must two putt par five's to make birdies. Wrong! If we golfers kept records on how many times we actually put the ball on the putting surface versus the times we get into trouble, we would not make such stupid mistakes. Recall what I said earlier about opinions in regard to planning your shot? Coming to the conclusion that two-putt birdies are better than one-putt birdies when the odds are against your placing the ball on the green in two is not sound thinking. A well-rounded golfer has the ability to putt and chip effectively, thus reducing the temptation to add undone pressure to other parts of his game. My shot was over 250 yards and into a strong wind. I didn't even have a good lie. Poor planning on my part.

Begin each pattern by standing behind the ball. Then complete your planning. To insure that your weight is on your right side, walk to the ball with your left shoulder higher than your right. Hands up front, position yourself to the ball, pick a specific target, align your body to it, shoulders first, feet second, and pull the "trigger." To bring the target closer to you, line up and imagine a line from the ball to the target. Within a couple of feet pick out a spot along that line and hit over it. **Stay in motion.** Ignore everything and everybody but the business at hand, which is to hit the ball correctly and let your stroke place the ball where you want it to go.

Mr. White sometimes showed me his pattern and reminded me of the use of the three "P's" saying, "Do I give the appearance that I know what I'm doing? Do I look positive?" There is a big difference between having a pattern and not having one.

POSITION

In Al Barkow's book, *Gettin' to The Dance Floor* there is a story of a set-up by Jack Burke, Jr. that made a lasting impression on me.

"Put it this way. In the earlier days of man, the hunter came out of the trees to get the deer. Now, he has to be very well-balanced. I wouldn't send a clumsy man after the deer. Would you? If I were a tribe leader I'd send a man who wouldn't step on branches and run the deer away. So in golf, when a guy steps up and looks like a machine he will not beat you. The guy who steps up there and has a waggle that looks natural, his timing looks natural, and he goes all the way around the course looking the same, he's the one who's going to beat you. When he gets on the putting surface he doesn't look like an octopus falling out of a tree. When he grabs the putter it almost looks like he has the driver in his hands. He doesn't look out of place anywhere. He's a very relaxed player."

The act of beginning to play a golf shot is called addressing the ball—or one's "set-up." At this point, you already know that in your mind there must be a very clear picture of the manner and direction in which you intend to play. As you approach the ball and stand before it, preparing to swing, arrange your posture so that you feel capable of delivering a blow along the desired path. You must sense your ability before the swinging of the club can have a purpose. "There should not be any effort to fit the stance to a prescribed diagram. Instead, consideration should be given to an overall awareness of the proper positioning."–Bobby Jones

Set your stance up to the ball so your swing will have maximum effectiveness. After you have the grip, and walk up to the ball, you will be able to determine the correct distance from the ball to place your feet. Remember, the ball should only be a comfortable distance away, permitting the arms to extend out to meet the shaft of the club. Poor posture, slouching, and tenseness have no place in addressing the ball. Many people, including the greatest golfer of all times, make the mistake of tucking their chin down at address. **Stand tall.** Mr. White told me to visualize a West Point soldier: walk tall and stand tall. He said, "The largest problem I ever had was getting people to stand tall at the ball."

The first time I heard this advice we were on the practice tee and I was having trouble making a sufficient shoulder turn on the backswing. Mr. White said that I needed to stand taller, with my head up and turned to the right. Before I knew it, my head was so far up that I could not see the ball. After bringing this to Mr. White's attention, I was told to lower it just enough to look down my nose at the ball. After lowering, I still could not see my feet. This was to train me to "stand tall." You don't have to stand this tall, but you must stand up. This point may cause many errors if overlooked. A restricted turn and moving out in front of the downswing are directly related to head position. Remember what I said earlier. I had lifted weights, causing my shoulders and neck muscles to be abnormally tight.

The address position should be one of ease, comfort, and relaxation. More than anything else, the finish posture must be one from which movement of the swing starts smoothly without having to break down successive barriers of tension caused by taut or strained muscles. The muscles and joints should be at ease in their movements.

For some nineteen years Nicklaus has constantly made reference to his set-up, weight, and head position. He never comes right out and says exactly what he has corrected, but I know by observing that they are the same problems I have struggled with: setting up too much over the ball instead of behind it, and having head down, thus restricting my ability to get back. This caused me to get too far out in front on the way down, making me come over the ball.

Since the position at impact is similar to the one you will take at the start of the backswing, it is very important that you get all parts of your body set-up in the correct position before any action takes place. The correct action of the swing is the natural outcome of the set-up position.

As in all athletics, good footwork and balance is vital to good performance. Athletes are built from the ground up, and the better player makes the most out of his connection with the ground. Proper footwork is fundamental in any golf shot. In placing your feet, your weight should be on the inside of the feet. Normally, your feet are shoulder width apart, narrowing only to stay consistent with the club being used, or only if you have chosen a fractional swing. However, the stance should be wide enough to support the turning of the body so that the weight stays on the inside of your feet, but not wide enough to restrict turning. The toes should be square to slightly open, and I do mean slightly.

Turning the left foot out and the left knee too far will hinder you from turning far enough on the backswing. The knees should be flexed slightly, back straight, head up, and turned to the right slightly. The ball position may vary according to the type of shot you wish to play. As a rule, it is never played outside your left heel. You should not be reluctant to move the ball around in your stance to hit different shots. Also, on normal iron shots, try playing it near the middle.

The stance is not only positioning yourself to the ball so as to line yourself up to the target. It is the essential set for beginning the backswing.

Your backswing will be directly affected, either good or bad, by your set-up.

Your feet should be square or at 90 degree angles to the target line. However, if you turn one or both out ever-so-slightly to help you get comfortable, that's all right. Other than keeping the right knee in position, there is no intentional restriction to the hips turning. Tension is set up when the hips are locked—unable to turn easily. The body is prevented from moving smoothly and easily in the routine you have prescribed for it. This is what accounts for the majority of bad shots under tournament pressure. Nicklaus, Jones, and Snead have large hip turns. This enables career longevity and reduces the chance for lower back problems.

In order for the club to travel its maximum arc, the left arm should be straight at address. Extending your left arm helps you to have a uniform arc, which will give you a better chance of building a repeating swing than a player who bends his arm. The elbows usually stay the same distance apart throughout the majority of the swing. Normally, this distance is as close as you can put them at address without undue stress. The elbows might change their distance at the top of your backswing because of the right arm and shoulder pull up. However, this separation is not a conscious move. Let it happen if it does. The closeness of the elbows is essential in accelerating the clubhead—which I might add, hits the ball, not any part of your body or other part of the club. The foregoing statement may sound "silly," but there have been many things printed which contradict. During the swing the knees work together. This will be more easily accomplished if you pinch them in toward each other, especially the right knee. It helps to keep you on the ball and in the **"pocket."** Then, on the downswing it is in position to release toward the target—to add power and to fire the right side.

The set-up may seem somewhat deliberate. This is because it must be exact before you can correctly "trigger" your takeaway. It is deliberate only to the extent of being conclusive;

not by conscious thought, but as a result of countless hours of practice to make the movements continuous. The critical alignment factor is the shoulders. "Unless you make a deliberate effort not to, you will instinctively swing the club through the ball parallel to your shoulders, no matter where your feet may be aligned."—Jack Nicklaus

The left shoulder should be "high" at address. This keeps your head back and your weight on the right side. Mr. White said, "David, I don't think you can set up too 'bowed.' When your game goes to bits, try bowing up or bracing yourself up."

It is only natural to look at the ball in your attempt to hit it. However, most good golfers are merely aware of the location of the ball. No doubt they are seeing it during the entire swing, but they do not stare at it. An ordinary observation and awareness of its presence and location are sufficient.

I can hear Mr. White saying, "David, it goes back to what we have been working on. If you don't plan and go through your three 'P's,' how do you expect to set up the same each time? Then you hit one left, one right, and ask what you are doing wrong." I said something about my shoulders being closed at address and Buck said, "Then you haven't planned and gone through your three 'P's'."

The following checklist should be your **standard operating position, your S.O.P:**

1. Feet, shoulders, and hips square or parallel to your line of flight.
2. About 60% of your weight should be back on your right side, inside right foot.
3. Your hands should be slightly forward, in front of, or in line with the clubhead.

4. Both knees pinched in (especially the right). Very Important.

5. Your head up and turned to the right. A good guide is looking down through your right knee to your right foot.

6. Stand tall, back straight, no slouching.

7. Elbows more together than separated.

8. Arms extended, (especially the left).

9. Ball played near middle to inside left heel.

10. Left shoulder very high (bowed).

Your **S.O.P.** and your **three P's** set the stage for everything to come. If there is a problem, chances are it can be found here.

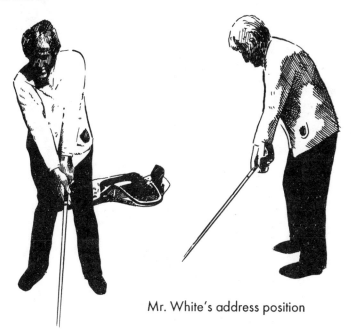

Mr. White's address position

Chapter **4**

The Swing

Does it Work and Will it Repeat?
Looks Don't Count
Don't Short Cut

"The **golf swing** is an art. To master this art it should first be reduced to a science, based on facts and data gathered from analysis along sound geometric, physical, mechanical, dynamic, and psychological lines and a theory should be evolved which covers every point, and which can be proved to be correct."–Seymour Dunn

THE BACKSWING

To successfully execute any golf shot you must **"trust your swing."** This trust comes from "believing" in yourself and having "faith" that what you know is sufficient to hit the shot. In many pressure situations a phrase from the Bible comes to mind; *O ye of little faith . . . .* To me this means that all failures have this in common. So I say to myself: "Have faith in yourself and your swing. Choose the swing you know how to make and go from there." This gives me the peace of mind to go ahead with the shot—peace of mind born from confidence that gives me the proper poise.

Some great golfers use what we call a "forward press" to help them trigger their takeaway:

1   moving the hands forward,

2   kicking the right knee in,

3   turning the right hip slightly forward.

Whatever you do, make sure that through addressing the ball and starting the club back you **"stay in motion."**

As I said earlier, it is the function of the pre-shot routine to insure constant movement. The movement that links the pre-shot routine with the beginning of the backswing is the "waggle." In order to waggle correctly the clubhead must be felt on the end of the shaft. Recall what I said earlier about a correction Mr. White made in my takeaway. Before this was brought to my attention, I started back with a slight lateral shift of the hips. This moved my hands and the handle of the club laterally, thereby leaving the clubhead behind. This was just the opposite of Mr. White's method, and he wasted no time in making sure I did it his way. Let me illustrate. The next time you go into your pro shop and examine a club—notice what you do. As you hold the club for inspection, you generally give the clubhead a little waggle so as to test the spring in the shaft and to feel the weight of the clubhead. During this examination I have never seen anyone test the club by shifting their hips or by wiggling the handle while leaving the clubhead on the floor. That is precisely what you are doing at this juncture of the pre-shot routine. By waggling the clubhead you are rehearsing the movement to come and exciting your senses by feeling the club. If you are right-handed, it is the one that should be in control of this movement. The function of the waggle and the movement of the body preceding the actual beginning of the backswing is to avoid or destroy tension in the position from which the swing is to make its start. Smoothness is an essential quality of the correct golf swing, and since a smooth start cannot be made if the muscles are taut or the posture strained, it is of the utmost importance that a player be relaxed and comfortable as he addresses the ball.

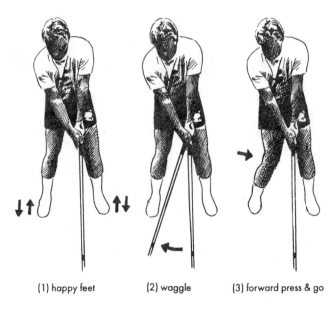

(1) happy feet   (2) waggle   (3) forward press & go

These three essential qualities will contribute more to your success than any attempt to learn the swing. Some of the greatest golfers I know shuffle their feet around or pat them up and down as they settle into their shots—Lee Trevino, Buck White, Bob Cornette, and John McGough just to name a few. Likewise, we should acquire the waggle of Tom Watson or Ben Hogan and the forward press of Gary Player.

A golf swing is made up of a series of movements that are mutually connected. In retrospect, I am convinced that Mr. White believed (and he is right), that in playing any golf shot there is only one sequence of movements.

Learning the backswing consists of getting a few movements clear in your mind, then learning to execute them. The only way to do this is to recall the correct feel of how the movements are produced. To make a correct takeaway and carry the swing on into the backswing you must be already (set-up) so that you may execute consistently. Without the correct set-up your chances of beginning are merely that, a chance. I have found that keeping two things in mind are all that is needed for swinging—one going back and one coming down. Although you may have to learn a great deal before you become an accomplished golfer, in the end one can only think of a couple of keys that trigger your swing. It is not possible to think through the entire swing when playing each shot.

The takeaway requires a sense of organization and a fair control of muscular action. Although at first this may require some thought, with persistent practice of the right hand it should become instinctive. The expert golfer already has his mind made up before his takeaway begins—then he lets his muscles do the work. After you have set up to the ball, the first move in beginning the takeaway is to turn the right side while swinging the clubhead back with the right hand and the right shoulder pull-up. By "side," I mean right shoulder, right torso, and right hip. The correct backswing originates with a turn of the body away from the ball. If you feel one aspect of the turn not cooperating, do not hesitate to accent the part that is lagging behind. You must **clear** the path the arms and club are to take to insure the correct plane.

As you begin the backswing in a one-piece motion the leg, foot, and hip movements are completed long before wrists, hands, and arms reach the top, and before the clubhead begins its return journey. Since you must keep your feet, legs,

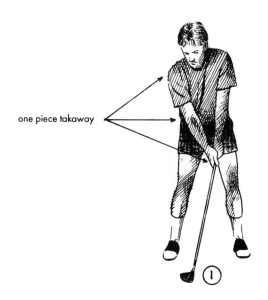

one piece takaway

Mr. White contended that the clubhead moves first on the backswing. This motion is initiated by the right hand, which causes the right wrist to begin hinging. The simultaneous movement of the right shoulder and right hip provides proper supervision over the clubhead and insures a one piece takeaway.

and hips moving smoothly, they get far ahead of the clubhead's completed journey. Allowing the arms and club to be pulled away like this helps to establish a more consistent backswing. The clubhead is moved by the cocking of the right hand off the ball and the swinging back of the right arm which is connected to the right shoulder. I suppose this is why I have always found it easier to turn my right shoulder than my right hip. However, **under no circumstances leave the right hip behind**.

"David, do you ever get 'hung' up on your backswing?" is a question Mr. White asked me many times before I finally answered, "Yes." He said the reason this happens is that my hands move laterally, causing my hips and shoulders to slide, instead of turning. "David, I never said you push anything away. Pushing on the backswing indicates using the left side and that's **not** part of my method. The right side is the side we are going to use. If I take my right hand and swing the club back, isn't the right hip going to turn? When the hips turn, the shoulders go along. 'Where's the hang-up? Can I be positive?' Allow the left heel to come up and left knee to cock back to insure less restriction in your turn."

When Mr. White moved the clubhead, his wrist started hinging immediately. This, along with the right hip turning, will not only start the club back correctly, but also help keep you in the **"pocket."** I have never mastered this part of my golf swing as well as the other parts. Like Mr. White, there have been many great golfers who brake off the ball quickly, namely: Bobby Locke, Dave Hill, Lanny Watkins, Hubert Green, Johnny Miller, and Tom Watson. As you turn your right hip away from the ball, it starts opening up your right side. In studying the greatest golfers, I have noticed that when they turn their bodies to the right, they pivot upon the right hip. When they turn to the left, they pivot upon the left hip. This indicates a shifting of weight from one side to another. Because you are, for the most part, seemingly turning in barrel, this is accomplished without noticeably moving your head. To pivot on the right hip, you must have the greater part of your body weight on the right side. Since you are trying to simplify and be efficient, begin (as Mr.White has said), with most of your weight already there.

As the right side turns and the right wrist hinges, the clubface will begin to open. Do not roll your hands over—just let it happen. The golf swing is an opening-closing motion of the clubface. The opening right side will begin a stretching action in the side and through the chest. This is due to the rotation motion caused by the right knee being fixed in, and staying in the pocket.

Like I said earlier, when I was stretching my right side back, I not only was loosening the tight muscles, but also was setting the stage for the sequence to come. I can also stretch my right side by turning the right shoulder back all the way. If I have trouble coordinating with the clubhead-hip takeaway, I often go to the clubhead-shoulder takeaway. Sometimes after practicing for a long period of time I will tire. When this happens, I am probably swinging too hard and getting nowhere.

While playing the eighth hole at the Broadwater Sea Course I hooked a drive far to the left. Mr. White's comment was, "David, you're 'forcing' the backswing; that means the club is going back too fast and your body can't catch up. Slow down and let your right hip and shoulder go back when the clubhead moves. David, I'll say it again, why did you hit it out? It's because you failed to make a backswing. **The club might get back but you didn't.** You should work harder on tempo. Coordinate your hands and arms with your turn.

Either turn faster or swing slower. Slow it down and **feel your turn"**

In so far as the hips are concerned, there should never be any lateral movement. They should turn just as though they were in a **"barrel."** The turn of the right hip will pull the left knee inward into position at the top. There is a tendency to leave the hips behind on the backswing. Not making a full body turn (don't get back) is one of the most common faults in golf. **Never restrict the hips from turning.**

Keep your right knee fixed in position, your weight on the inside of your right foot. Then turn them as far as they can go. If I am pulling most of my shots to the left, or cutting across the ball instead of hitting straight, I look at the hip turn as the likely trouble spot. You may find that you have restricted yourself from making a proper hip turn on the backswing, and on the downswing **you** are "sliding" your hips laterally toward the target too much, instead of turning them. Both faults will occur at the expense of power and accuracy. Most golfers are right-handed, so it's often easier to think in right-handed terms. **On the backswing, therefore, concentrate specifically on turning the right hip away from the ball.**

Thinking of it this way makes the movement seem less complicated and easier to accomplish correctly. Be sure to turn the right hip far enough so that the left hip and left shoulder have rotated enough. Many great golfers have shoulder turns of a hundred degrees and hip turns of fifty degrees.

The turn of the body has little meaning, unless the feet maintain a positive grip upon the ground. There can be little question that the turn of the hips and shoulders, and the balancing of this turn upon the feet and legs, is the essence of effective form. Footwork, like everything else in the golf swing, should be perpetual. (Remember what I said about staying in motion.) It is this continuous, unaudited feel that sets up a flow of power. You can only turn from the inside with your hips and shoulders on the downswing if you keep your feet moving continuously ahead of the hips and shoulders. This enables you to turn your hips inside and behind the ball: behind both in position and in the proper sequence.

On the backswing the arc is established by the extension of the left arm. This extension is from the tip of your left shoulder to the end of your left hand knuckles, not from shoulder to clubhead. If that occurs, there will be no wrist break at the top of your swing and the club will be pointing straight up in the air. The arc should be extended as far as possible without causing too much undue stress.

The wider the arc, the more room is provided, developing power in striking the ball. The stretching from golf movements, from the feet up through the body, and down through arms and hands, are felt as one "feel, — the feel when we swing the club **wide** back, through the ball, and around the left side. The correct turning of the hips enables this feel to be maintained and consistent. The feel of the clubhead being a long way from the ball, a long way from your left side, spinal column, and sternum, is a most desirable one.

It is very important to remember this feel. If you can widen the gap between the clubhead and your left side, do so. It is almost impossible to get it too wide. "The gap means that you are coming down one after another." –Percy Boomer

If you liken the backswing of a golf club to the extension of a coil spring, or the stretching of a rubber band, you will be right on the mark. The greater the extension of stretching, the greater the force of the return. In a golf swing, every inch

This illustration shows how the right side opens up during the backswing and by clearing a path encourages the arms and club to follow.

added to the backswing windup (up to the limit at which the balance of the body can be easily maintained), represents additional stored energy available to increase the power of the downswing. As a result of this extension, the left arm will remain almost perfectly straight in the backswing.

The left arm will extend far enough if the right arm is allowed to function naturally. **The right arm pull-up induces the left arm stretch.** Also, as long as your shoulders turn, you will have good extension. Your left arm will only break down if your shoulders prematurely stop turning. If you feel wide as you go up (and you should), your arm will be straight. Your left arm is kept straight to give you a wide swing so that your clubhead will come in from behind the ball at a lesser angle than had it come from above.

Do not pull down with your arms. Pull down from your legs and left side. If you start the downswing by grounding your left heel, the rest of your body, shoulders, and arms, being reactive, will respond to this pull from the leg. Your arms and hands will be started down slowly and quietly—to gather speed as they get down behind the back of the ball.

As the right arm pulls back and up, the left arm stretches. This sets up a natural leverage action between the hands, which will induce the wrists to "cock" fully. This cocking should start from the beginning. One of the best ways to convince yourself to use an earlier cocking action of the hands

The backswing is dominated by the right hand, arm and shoulder pull up. As in other sports, as my good friend Steve DeBerg demonstrates, when these muscles are fully induced it is natural for the arm to come away from the body.

(on the backswing should be right side oriented), is to swing the club with one hand at a time.

Turn your right shoulder back as far as possible against the resistance of the right leg foundation and the right knee. Make sure your head stays in position. If you pull the right shoulder back all the way, your right elbow is surely going to come away from your body at the top (flying elbow). That is all right. The only way the right shoulder can be brought to the correct position at the top of the backswing is to activate the muscles of that shoulder, insuring that the right shoulder blade is drawn back to its fullest extent at the top of the swing. Since there is no way possible for the left arm, hand, and side to take the club much past hip level, the right hand, arm, hip and shoulder must take over in order to get it back to the top. If this is the case, which I believe it is, why not start with the right side from the beginning?

One of the most overlooked sources of power in a golf-swing is the knees, especially the right knee. The hips, knees, and feet all work together in creating power, but the knees serve as the focal point. The right knee becomes the critical point of the entire swing. It should remain in position, and not move during the backswing. Just rotate around the right knee, and keep it flexed, in order to avoid it straightening up against the pressure generated by the right hip turning and the right shoulder pulling up. This is something I continue to work on now, as I did in my early sessions with Mr. White.

When it is braced in this fashion, the body coils like a spring around the knee. This firmness builds up power for the downswing. It also makes it impossible to lose power by swaying away from the ball. As the right side begins turning, the left knee will be pulled in toward the right knee and behind the ball. Mr. White told me one time that when he won the Memphis Open, he thought of it as "touch–touch." What he meant was that on the backswing the left knee would touch the right, and the opposite on the downswing. If the left heel is pulled off the ground by the turning of the right side and the cocking of the left knee, let it happen. This is what we want it to do. Remember, the backswing is turning the stretching. The windup has to be made with the weight on the right foot. To achieve this consistently, it's best to start with most of your weight there.

Winding up the right arm and wrist is essential in most athletic actions; and golf is no exception. The setting of the right hand so that the shaft points over the top of the right shoulder is also vital, since it insures that you are swinging in the right plane. The back of the left hand, wrist, and forearm should form a straight line at the completion of the backswing. However, as important as this is, it does not override the importance of hinging. So, if you cannot hinge enough, it is all right to cup the left wrist a little.

Since golf is a game of fingers and hands working in coordination with other parts of the body, the best swing in the world is only as good as one's strength. The fingers should be strong enough to hinge going back and hang on the club at impact. If your hands are weak, the shock of impact will move them on the club. Strength might not be essential for playing golf, but try playing without it.

Jack Nicklaus said, **"Completing the backswing** is one of the best mental pictures I know to develop tempo and consistent rhythm, especially in bad weather or when faced with a particularly difficult shot." When you are under pressure for any reason, it is easy to "start down before you've gotten back all the way" There is no noticeable pause between the backswing and the downswing. They should flow into each other.

The "plane" is a line that runs from the ball through your shoulders. The swing is not straight back; it is inside where the shoulders take it. The hands and wrists yield in authority to the pivot; they are not allowed to determine direction. They do not decide in which direction they should go; they go in the arc set out for them by the turning of the pivot. This is true of the upswing as well as the downswing. The pivot not only provides the power, it also controls direction—guiding the clubhead in its correct plane through the ball. The further straight back you go, the further off the plane you go.

Undoubtedly you would like the club at the top of your backswing to be parallel to the line of flight. However, many good golfers (so called) "cross the line" at the top. Those players are fortunate enough to have long, full backswings that generally cross the line. Let your right hand go where your right shoulder takes it. You should not make a conscious effort to get the club parallel to the ground. When done correctly, you will have your hands full just getting back this far. If you coil further, go ahead. Hold onto the club, keep your head still, and keep your right knee fixed in position.

The head should be steady throughout the backswing since, if it moves, the body does too, disturbing the club's path. The steady head assures you the balance you must have to allow the body to move properly. If your head is to be kept steady, your body must turn on a pivot. Conversely, if you move your head, you ruin body motion.

Cocking the head like a forward press is a positive move to start the backswing. This makes it possible to take a longer, freer turn with the whole body than would be possible if the head were held straight to the front. Most important, it is a method by which we help brace ourselves against swaying to the left on the downswing, and at impact, moving our body out ahead of the ball. If it did one more thing, it would be to help your right hand release through the ball. One time Mr. White told me my head was moving out in front on the downswing. At the time, I never lost sight of the ball. Do not make this mistake. Because you don't lose sight of the ball doesn't mean that you haven't moved your head.

I asked Buck what his last thought was before swinging the club back. He said, "Just take the right hand and swing back—two waggles, and go. This allows one to be positive and stay in motion." This explains why I spent so much time over the ball. While over the ball, you can't take two waggles and also think how to swing the club.**Swing the club back. Don't place it.**

$\Leftarrow$
Start Position
(The Swing-side view #1)

⇐ Right side leads the way—highlighted by the turning of the right hip as the clubhead is swung a long way from the center axis. (The Swing-side view #2)

The right shoulder muscles are fully activated to bring the club to the top, producing a tremendous stretching sensation down the left side. (The Swing-side view #3) ⇒

⇐ Lower body races to get ahead beginning from the ground up. The right elbow is drawn up against the right side so the blow can be delivered from the inside. (The Swing-side view #4)

Left hip clears out of the way as you come
square against the back of the ball.
(The Swing-side view #5

The right side has fully released
through to the target.
(The Swing-side view #6)

Address position
(The Swing-front view #1)

The club is swept away in one piece.
(The Swing-front view #2)

Right arm, right shoulder pull up is being
fully activated producing full extension
of the left arm and a stretching motion
down the left side.
(The Swing-front view #3)

At the top the weight is predominately
on the right side—back is facing target,
poised and ready to fire.
(The Swing-front view #4)

⇐ The lower body begins weight transfer.
Right elbow becomes visible and is
drawn in close to the side.
(The Swing-front view #5)

Hips clear leading the way, left shoulder ⇒
moves upwards, head remains behind ball,
and right side releases through impact.
(The Swing-front view #6)

⇐ The left side stretches up as right side
continues through.
(The Swing-front view #7)

⇐
Momentum has carried you up to the top.
Weight is predominately on the left side.
Remember to stand tall.
(The Swing-front view #8)

THE DOWNSWING

There are many different methods and much speculation about how to start the downswing. Dropping the left heel, kicking the left knee forward, turning the left hip out, and shifting your weight forward by pushing off the right foot, are some of the moves that have proven successful for many of golf's greatest players. As for me, **stretching my left side** seems to provide the proper sequence of movements and produces consistent feel that enables me to return to the ball properly. The downswing starts with the left heel returning to the ground. This reacts on the legs, hips, and shoulders to produce the centrifugal sweep of the clubhead. Although by listing these movements separately I am indicating a sequence of movements. When a good swing starts down, everything ought to move together toward the ball. I define this left side stretching motion by calling it "left-shoulders/left-heel" separation. I want to stretch upward against the ground with my left leg and foot—gradually and without haste. The push against the ground causes my left side to stretch, which opposes the pull of the clubhead.

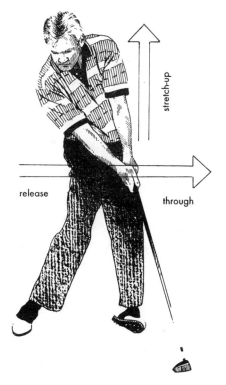

The left shoulder stretching up provides a solid wall to hit against. Much intensity is added to the right side release by bracing up. Most great golfers I have observed have very high left shoulders during impact.

⇐ All golf is in a state of opposition. Just as this olympic hammer thrower creates a state of opposition by having his body oppose the pull of the ball, so do we oppose the clubhead by "bracing up" and staying in the "pocket."

"All golf is opposition. We are in a state of opposing in every phase of our swing; even in the waggle. The very feel of the clubhead is only sensed when we are in a state of opposition to it."—Percy Boomer

The more you can stretch up from the ground, the more you can feel down from the shoulders. This is what I try to feel beyond everything else. Since at the top of my backswing my left shoulder is under my chin and my left heel is off the ground, it is logical to think of a separation between these two as setting up a stretching motion. One of the things I admired most about Mr. White's style of play was how well he stayed up through the swing. To have the feeling that you are staying up, you need to stretch down through your arms as you come into contact with the ball, then find something to stretch against. In other words, you have to stretch up from the feet to set up the necessary resistance in the shoulders. You have to brace the top of your swing by giving it something to pull against; otherwise you cannot stretch firm down from it. Fix the top end by bracing and stretching up to hold your shoulders firmly in place.

At this point, I confess that I have no more feel for my left heel than I do for reciting Homer's "Iliad and Odyssey." Although Mr. White has constantly made reference to the left heel going down as being the first move in the downswing, I have to rely on my left side stretching to accomplish this. I am, however, capable of pushing off from my right foot, knee, and hip. This returns my left heel to the ground and initiates the transfer of my weight toward the left side. Likewise, I am capable of working with my left knee, hip, and shoulder to accomplish the same thing. I find it far more effective to think of these movements as a "whole," rather than singling out any one movement. If you drop the left heel, you must activate something else to help bring the club down. If you turn your left hip, it may also induce your left shoulder to open too soon, causing your weight to stay back. One thing for certain: pulling down with your left hand will not activate any other part of your body—except your left arm.

The uncoiling of the body is not initiated by the arms. No matter how perfect the backswing may have been, if the hands, or the arms start the downswing, the club inevitably loses the guidance the body movement could have provided and the benefit of the power the muscles of the waist and back could have contributed. The head and shoulders should not accompany the hips in the initial movement. Done correctly, the body will lead, setting up a sequence of movements starting from the ground up. Stretching the left side on the downswing makes the left heel go down, the left knee kick out, initiates the weight transfer, causes the left hip to turn, the left shoulder to return upwards, and hence, insures that the arms and hands follow.

In any full swing, correctly performed, the body will begin its return journey while the hands and club are still going back. These movements have the effect of accomplishing two very important results. First, it makes the lower body movements usable in the form of clubhead speed. Secondly, and equally important, is the effect of completing the cocking of the wrists. This is accomplished as the wrists give to the pull of the hips, legs and foot movement in one direction, and of the clubhead moving in the other. This was illustrated in Bobby Jones' tapes, entitled *How I Play Golf.* **As the downswing begins, you should have the feeling of leaving the clubhead at the top.** You delay while at the same time you are beginning the downswing. "We are waiting in movement." –Percy Boomer

A baseball player's swing further identifies the qualities of a good golf swing.
(1) The batter is poised and ready to strike with his weight back and on the inside of his right foot.
(2) The lower body initiates the weight transfer while the bat stays back and the hinging angle increases.
(3) The hips clear the way as right elbow leads and is returned closed to the side.
(4) The release is saved until the bat is in the hitting area.

One characteristic a golf swing should have is smoothness. As the downswing begins, the acceleration must be sequential; the motion must be unhurried and free from any sudden or jerky movements. You can best accomplish it in this manner. Allow the clubhead plenty of time to gather speed before it reaches the ball. The downswing is intended to culminate in a well-timed, powerful square contact between clubhead and ball. Do not overlook the fact that the backswing has to establish a perfectly-balanced, powerful position at the top of the swing, from which the correct movements of the downswing can flow into the stroke without the need for interference or correction. In the end, the movements that introduce the downswing become just as important as the actual hitting—the entire swing, a sequence of correct positions following comfortably one after the other.

The left shoulder going up insures that your head will stay back and your right side will stay low through the shot. The proper weight shift is a shift of the hips—a lateral movement of the middle part of the body that does not alter the location of the head and shoulders with respect to the ball. Although there is no doubt that the weight shift does occur, Mr. White believed that in the beginning of the downswing, there is no significant weight transfer to the left side, which during impact would cause the majority of your weight to be on the left leg and in front of the ball.

Instead, most of your weight (more than 50%) stays on the inside of the right leg and behind the ball where your head is. In the case of most great golfers, the head is located over the right knee at time of impact. The better you stretch, the better you will stay behind the ball and "in the pocket" to avoid getting out in front too early. Golfers actually move their heads back and down a bit, so there's a good chance your left shoulder and left hip will not return as far forward as they were at the set-up. Stretching the left side will also stop your wrist from unhinging too early, thus saving them for power at the ball.

As the downswing begins, the strength contained by the right knee is released by pushing off the inside of the right foot. This will cause the right knee to turn in toward the target. The side that delivers the power—the right side—is put into position to deliver by correct footwork. As the right side springs into action from the right foot up, the left heel will simultaneously go to the ground. It helps to roll on the inside of the right foot, since this will help keep your right side low instead of coming up too soon on your right toe. Good examples of this are early pictures of Sam Snead.

As stated earlier, there is no pronounced "lateral shift of the hips" initiating the downswing. If you move your hips too much laterally, this will in turn force your head and trunk to also move laterally. Then your whole upper body will get in front of the ball at impact, and you will be trying to do the impossible—hit a ball that is behind you. Mr. White said, "Hitting a golf ball is like hitting any other ball, in that it cannot be hit hard or effectively if it is behind the hitter." By mentioning the negative role of the hips in this manner I, by no means, wish to be disrespectful. No other motion is so critical to a successful swing than that of correct hip movement. The hips being lower than the shoulders and closer to the ground must be started first so that they can get ahead. As we come down and through the ball, the inward turning of the ball requires great muscular activity in the feet, calves and thighs. This generates power in the golf swing. It is this controlled movement of the hips that applies this power smoothly and gradually in the correct direction. You must incorporate into your swing, through repetitive practice, hip movement which you can control by a definite feel. By activating this feel, you can control the degree and direction of power in your swings.

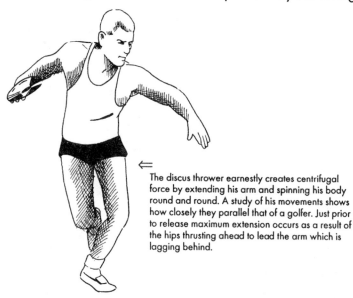

⇐ The discus thrower earnestly creates centrifugal force by extending his arm and spinning his body round and round. A study of his movements shows how closely they parallel that of a golfer. Just prior to release maximum extension occurs as a result of the hips thrusting ahead to lead the arm which is lagging behind.

Since the downswing is led by the stretching and clearing of the left side, complete use is made of the power in the player's legs and back muscles. Lifting your left shoulder causes your left arm to straighten completely as it comes down into position. The long hitter gets his body in position so his hands can work effectively. If the hands and arms get ahead of the unwinding of the hips, knees, and shoulders, the tension is lost, and the power in the larger muscles will be lost. Thanks largely to the wrist lagging behind, the speed of the clubhead is several times greater than the speed of the hands and arm pull. **As the downswing begins, don't be in a hurry to hit the ball.** In golf the ball is stationary, so don't attempt to hit the ball until you get in the hitting area.

As closely as I can, I will describe the sensation of striking the golf ball. It is a combination of stretching through the ball with the left side combined with a hitting action of the right hand and forearm. The left side is responsible for keeping the swing on track or in the groove, and the right side is the agent responsible for bringing the movement to a well-timed release as the ball is struck.

If, at the moment of impact, you stop the forward pull and stretching of the left side (which is what you will do if you focus your attention at the ball), the power you have generated is not available and the clubhead cannot (as it should) continue accelerating through the ball until the ball is well on its way. Many of the great shots I have made have occurred when I had the feeling that I had stayed in contact with the ball for a long time. If you stop the forward pull and stretching of the left side at the moment of impact with the ball, this sets up the resistance necessary to take up the shock during contact. At the same time, you should keep the clubhead accelerating through the ball. If you let up on the forward pull when you strike the ball, you stop the acceleration of the clubhead at the ball. You will have committed a gross error in swinging. "That is why **we should never try to hit the ball. Cultivate a sweep through the ball, and let the ball be nothing more than in the way.**"—Percy Boomer

During the swing, it is good to feel the right hand and right shoulder come square against the back of the ball. Learn that although your eyes are on the ball at the moment of impact, your sight is not focused on it; the ball is merely on the fringe of your attention. Your mind's attention is always concentrated on where you want the ball to go. Of course, you know that you are not free to move your head until after impact. Even then, it is not a conscious move; but is forced to come up because of the momentum in the stroke and the coming through of the right shoulder.

In the throwing position, the elbow is seen to lead the way before the arm is extended towards its target. On the downstroke, the right elbow that was drawn away from the side on the backswing now leads the way as the wrist remains fully locked, close to the side.

The correct stroke causes the clubhead to appoach the ball from inside the line of play. Mr. White said, "The swing must remain on the player's side of the ball." Of course, this would not be possible unless the return stroke was originated from the ground up. The correct shift of the hips and transfer of weight during the downstroke maintains a bend in the right arm that keeps the right elbow close to the side of the body. The stretching of the left side dominates the strong pull of the left arm through the swing. One of the greatest baseball pitchers of all time, Nolan Ryan, said that so far back as he could remember he learned that the fundamental in pitching was to "lead with your elbow." These factors insure that at the moment of impact the hands should be on a line with or ahead, of the clubhead, and that the left hand should carry through the ball without beginning to turn.

The majority of players, who fail in manufacturing power, do so because their left hand fails to act as a fulcrum for the right hand to strike against. The left hand has to resist against the right. This point was stressed to me several times during my meetings with Mr. White. One of the best illustrations of this is found in Seymour Dunn's book, *Golf Fundamentals*. He wrote:

"To understand this matter, take a club in your hands and press the face of it against the inside of a door frame with enough force to bend the shaft. Maintain this pressure and ask yourself, 'What am I doing with the upper palm of my left hand?' You will discover that you are very decidedly pressing the club handle backward against the forward pressure of your right hand. Take the left hand away and try to maintain the same bend in the club shaft and you will at once be convinced.

This back pressure of the left hand must be done at the moment of impact if you are to overcome the resistance of the ball. If you fail to do this, the club handle may go there, but the clubhead will come dangling along behind with very little emphasis through the hit."

⇐ One of the best mental images I know of is hitting against an imaginary wall. The thought of the clubface, palm of the right hand, and the back of my left hand coming square up against the back of a wall, helps heighten my senses of a square hit down the target line.

"There is no doubt in my mind that the right hand and arm have to hit and hit hard," said Ben Hogan. The hands must hit past the body due to the extension of the arms. The release of the right hand gradually turns down and over as the right hand hits past it (but not till after impact). The action is rolling, releasing, and turning of the hands, not an inward collapsing of the left wrist or a forward bending of the right wrist. An "inside-out" clubhead path helps accentuate this. You may think of releasing the right hand as "turning two knuckles down" in the left hand. Mr. White said that he used this term earlier in his career. I remind you that **nothing is automatic.**

You must make it happen. You don't get something for nothing. To emphasize this further, let me relate this story.

One day at Pinehurst, North Carolina, Miller Barber, who is considered to be a notorious right to left player, was hitting balls on the range. Apparently, he was leaving the ball out to the right, and after several frustrating passes he left the range to seek out Mr. White, whom he'd seen earlier. "Buck," he said, "would you watch me hit some balls? I'm leaving everything to the right." Off they went. After observing a few swings, Mr. White said, "Miller, you need to release the right hand through impact." "I thought that was automatic," said Miller. White retorted, "If it were automatic, then what am I doing here?" A point you and I would do well to learn.

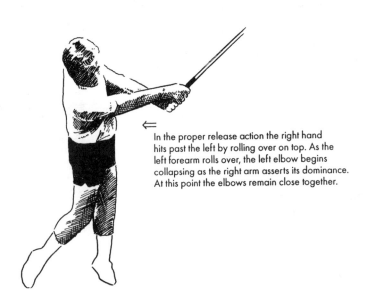

In the proper release action the right hand hits past the left by rolling over on top. As the left forearm rolls over, the left elbow begins collapsing as the right arm asserts its dominance. At this point the elbows remain close together.

A player must acquire sufficient confidence and faith in the swing to resist making a last-minute correction (manipulation) or addition on the ball itself. "I believe that the impulse to steer, born from negative thoughts, is ccountable for almost every bad shot. The sad fact is that no amount of steering can possibly do any good, and it may serve to magnify errors." –Bobby Jones

What a pity. Had we just resisted our desire to hit at the ball and concentrated our efforts upon producing the proper swing: power generated from the hips, shoulders controlled by feet movement, arms, reacting to the bracing up of shoulders, and wrist free to strike, we would have sent it far down the fairway and straighter. When steering comes into your mind, it may be in the form of begging, such as "Please let me . . . ." You can finish the sentence. To combat the negative, always remember the three "P's," trust your swing, and **accelerate the clubhead.** No matter how big or small the shot, always accelerate the clubhead. When you accelerate the clubhead through the ball, it will have a tendency to true itself up at impact. With a proper swing, the harder you hit, the better you'll hit it.

The follow-through is greatly enhanced by the momentum you have created. This turning, stretching, arm swing, hands, and club motion should carry you up to the top. Keep the left shoulder going.

To strike the ball correctly in a given direction requires these three essentials: (please turn page)

☞ The clubhead must strike the ball square in the back perpendicular to line of flight.

☞ The clubhead must be traveling in the direction of play during impact.

☞ The clubhead should be traveling at maximum speed.

At the finish the majority of your weight should be on your left side with the hands held high and your stomach facing the target. According to Mr. White, this position should resemble a West Point soldier.

Chapter **5**

Chipping

"Well David, I never did want to be the longest wedge player in the world."–Buck White

"The chip is the great economist of golf."–Bobby Jones

Pitching the ball

Pitching the ball, as the British say, can be some of the most gratifying golf you will ever play. In my education from Buck White University, I think I majored in chipping and minored in swinging. The reason I say this is because I spent the majority of my time learning how to get "up-and-down." The curriculum is very simple—you study basics. After eleven years of study I have my doctorate from BWU, and I consider it more valuable than one from Oxford, because I could have come closer to being accepted into that English institution than I would have into BWU. For all I know, I am the last person to receive a degree from this elite school.

There is sound logic behind advance chipping. If a player is very good in the art of chipping, he will not be worried when he misses a green. If that is the case, he will come closer to making a better swing from wherever he is at the time because he knows that he can "get it up and down." This relieves the pressure.

Before any shot, the first thing I do is check the lie of the ball. This tells me the type of shot I can or cannot play. Then I feed into my mental computer such things as: obstacles between me and the green, the speed of the green, the way the green runs, and the putt that remains. All this information can influence the choice of shot or selection of a target point. Finally, I visualize the length and type of swing that will do the job. The pitch shot is just a miniature version of the full swing, whether you make a 3/4, 1/2 or 1/4 swing. It requires a certain touch and feel. Mr. White described feel as "how much." You have to think through your carefully built-up sense of feel "how much" swing to make and "how hard" to make it. Remember the three "P's."

To have a good chipping game, you must aim to a spot, visualize the ball landing there and running up to the hole. In my eleven year (countless rounds of play and hundreds of hours of practice) association with Mr. White, I can honestly say that I do not remember a time in which he played a shot without giving it his undivided attention. I was impressed how that during his planning stage he literally stared at where he wanted the ball to go. There was no confusion or doubt as to how he was going to play the shot. Equally impressive was how he again held his pose after the execution of the stroke. He held this position until the ball came to rest. This ritual was consistent whether it be a chip shot or a complete swing. If I didn't know better, I'd think he was trying to intimidate the ball, as if to dare it not go in. Less successful golfers give a mere casual glance at their intended direction of play. They aim to a general rather than to a specific location. They do not look with conviction at a certain point where they want the ball to land. You cannot expect your eye to make an exacting register on your mind if you do not look in an exacting manner. Look at the ball, then look at the exact place where you want to send it. Then return your attention to the ball and hit it without delay before the eye loses its focus. Mr. White says, "One of the best lessons you will ever learn is turning three shots into two." He also has told me a thousand times to learn the importance of the "run-up" shot, and always in planning your shot to "play the percentages."

I have learned, on my run-up shots, that if I "cup" (close the clubface) a little, position the ball back in my stance, and close up a little going through by releasing my right hand, I am able to produce over-spin. The result is a truer roll. Remember to grip down on the club in order to drill the ball. There is a minimal amount of body turn. The hinge and a small arm motion is all that is necessary in such a short, firm stroke. The stretch I speak of often is taken care of in the proper set-up position. Throwing the ball up in the air is a great asset; yet, until you become proficient in the run-up shot, you will never be complete. The run-up-shot often reduces risk in a chip shot. It has the same effect as the "Texas wedge."

The set-up in chipping is, for all practical purposes, the same set-up as in your normal swing. Narrowing the stance and gripping down are the noticeable differences. According to Mr. White, the most common error is "getting out in front," when going through the ball. He also has told me, "I don't think you can play *de-accelerate;* you must *accelerate* the clubhead." If the head moves forward your elbows separate and the clubhead will de-accelerate. In review:

1. Set-up with your left shoulder very high to help prevent you from moving forward and putting your "pick" in the ground.

2. The stance is relative to the distance you wish to go.

3. The hips should be square to slightly open because they should turn with respect to the distance you take the club back.

4. The knees are pinched in toward each other, especially the right knee. They may even touch.

5. Remember to stand tall with your head up and turned slightly to the right.

6. Arms extended and hands forward.
Hands being forward will help eliminate "scooping." Unless your hands are set forward you will not be able to hinge correctly off the ball.

7. Your weight should be predominantly on your right side (about 65%).

8. The ball should be in the middle, not forward where you will have to **"chase"** it on your downswing.

9. Reach for the ball so your backswing will go slightly to the inside on the takeaway. You can also turn better and your right thigh will not be in the way.

10. Be firm and positive.

On the takeaway, move the clubhead and right hip together. The clubhead should begin to hinge from the start. As it does, it will go to the inside. Keep the extension in the left arm and stretch your right side. Width is important. **Clear back and clear through.** On your 3/4, 1/2 and 1/4 shots you will take your hands back to shoulder high, hip high, and thigh high level respectively. **"Load the gun"** by remembering to move your right hip and side when the clubhead moves. The right shoulder moves up. It does not move laterally nor does any other part of your right side. **I cannot overemphasize the importance of staying in the pocket.** To help him hinge more and get greater clubhead speed, I noticed that Mr. White used a modified ten finger grip. As he hinged, his right palm would often come away from the shaft at the top, leaving only his thumb and a couple of fingers holding on. This is something I think every senior should look into as he loses suppleness (Mr. White was a senior). Lately, I have started leaving the little finger of my right hand off the shaft as a practice device. I recommend this for people who need clubhead awareness.

On the downswing, start by stretching your left side up to the sky and extending the right forearm. The left side turning and stretching can be described as clearing. This clearing action, while going through the ball, adds width. The reason I mentioned two things is because on your smaller chips you will find it difficult to stretch. The swing is so small all you can do is hinge and unhinge by releasing the right forearm and releasing the right hand. On short chips you may find leaving your right heel on the ground will help you stay down and behind the ball. Keep your head back and release through the ball, not at it—accelerating the clubhead. The left arm and left wrist do not break down; rather, they remain firm to support the striking action of the right hand/forearm. In bad lies remember to play the ball further back, hinge, and really accelerate. Do not choke up on the club. Get the benefit of the total weight of the club.

In studying the punch of a karate instructor we find that as one arm is extended forward the opposite arm is retracted at the same time with almost identical emphasis. It can be said that the retraction of the front arm helps propel the opposite arm forward as the trunk maintains its original position. We see the same force applied to the spinning of a locomotive's wheels. The force in opposite directions causes the wheel to spin. This is entirely true with the down stroke of the golf swing. Whether a big swing or a small swing the pull of the left side up helps accentuate the release of the right side down and through.

To further emphasize his chipping method, Mr. White brought up this interesting point with respect to wedge play in 1/2 and 3/4 swings. "Have you ever seen anybody turn it (the clubhead) over too fast?" I have not. Instead, you see people trying to hit the ball with the handle and "shanking" it. Set-up like I have said with pressure in your grip in the three fingers of your left hand. Go through the method we have talked about. Set the club to the inside, and you will have your hands full trying to turn it over enough (so long as you stretch). Take a pitching wedge or sand wedge and back up from the green about forty yards. You will never see anyone hook the ball off the green with their best effort . . . done correctly. Keep the width in your swing. Your 3/4, 1/2 and 1/4 swings will go through just that far, shoulder high, hip high, and thigh level. Stay in the pocket. My sand wedge has 62 degrees loft (fifty-six degrees is standard). This helps me get the ball in the air more. "Well, David, I never did want to be the longest sand wedge player in the world." –Sir Buck, Lord of Chipping

Every time I think of a pitch shot rolling, I immediately have flashbacks to one day at the Broadwater Sea Course 19th hole while having lunch with Mr. White. This particular day the room was full of golfers having lunch and the tables were pushed closer together than normal. Sitting directly behind us was a group of regulars who had just finished their morning round. Frank, in a voice louder than normal, talked about his struggling chipping game and how he could not get the ball to stop. It was hard to determine whether he took offense with his ability or with the conditions of the greens. Because of the length of the conversation, I assume that it may have been to provoke Mr. White's attention. Having about all he could stand, Mr. White joined in the conversation by evoking two thought provoking questions.

"Frank," he said, "What shape is a golf ball?"

"Round," came the reluctant reply.

"Right," said Mr. White.

"Frank," asked Mr., White, "What's a round ball supposed to do?"

"Roll," said Frank.

After a slight pause as if to emphasize a point Mr. White said, "Right." End of conversation. For those of you who have not played golf in Mississippi in the summertime, it is very difficult if not impossible to pitch the ball from behind or from the sides of those small, elevated, old greens built sometime back in the 1920's.

SIX PRACTICE "KEYS"

1. Backswing—hinge so the clubhead is above your hip level and hands are below.

2. Downswing—release so the clubhead is above your hip level and hands below.

3. Left eye peer at the ball. Stare at the ball, until it stops rolling, as if to dare it to roll off line.
   After all, "What's a round ball supposed to do?"

4. Right side, left side clearing.

5. Practice playing shots standing on your right foot—only to become aware of lateral movement.

6. Swing through and hold.

⇐ Beginning position—hands forward,
right knee in and left shoulder high

Set angle early on the backswing
by moving clubhead and right
shoulder up together. ⇒

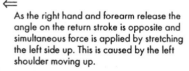

⇐ As the right hand and forearm release the
angle on the return stroke is opposite and
simultaneous force is applied by stretching
the left side up. This is caused by the left
shoulder moving up.

Chapter **6**

Sand Play

Good sand play starts with a good sand wedge.

Bunker play and wedge play are similar except for two aspects. First, in sand play stance is wider (dig in to get firm footing so you do not slip). Second, I accent the role my right hand and right arm play in the normal swing by swinging the club back and hinging more. Going through, I swing the clubhead beneath and through the ball by extending my right arm and releasing my right hand. I keep the swing long and slow, trying hard to maintain good rhythm and tempo. I stay in the pocket. I accelerate the clubhead. I avoid moving out in front on the way down, because that will cause me to de-accelerate and stick the "pick" in the sand.

The distance you want the ball to go is determined by two things:

1. How far behind the ball you hit.
2. How long and hard you swing.

Follow through unless you have a very bad lie or unless the lip of the bunker restricts you. On buried lies it may be helpful to move the ball back in your stance and close the clubface at address. This increases the angle of attack and allows the leading edge to dig, thereby decreasing the bounce of the club. Experiment with opening and closing the clubface at address. People are generally afraid of something they do not do often, so jump in there. You may find you like it.

The most valuable information on the fairway bunkers that Mr. White ever gave me was to "fix the right knee in." More often than not your backswing will be smaller than normal. Keep a good tempo and stretch through the ball. Extend the right arm and release the right hand. Remember the two pitfalls are:

1. not turning the right side on the backswing,
2. the head and body moving forward on the downswing, causing the clubhead to de-accelerate.

Practice when you get a chance. You may need more club. Be realistic. Many times you won't be able to hit the green. So do not try. Play percentages—never gamble.

Buck said that Snead was the best. He never played a round of golf that he did not hit at least ten or so bunker shots before commencing play.

Two of the best mental images I know of for producing good bunker shots are: (1) that of an airplane pilot practicing touch-and-go's, and (2) the underarm throwing motion needed to make a flat rock skip across a pond.

Chapter **7**

Wind Play

It's not illegal to cup it.
A good hard stretch.

This is a subject that players are overwhelmingly stubborn about. I have come to realize that a moderate wind provides a fine test of skill. The player, who best controls his ball and displays the most resourcefulness in overcoming the difficulties imposed by the wind, demonstrates his advantage. Together with putting, hitting into the wind was the primary reason that my tour performance was so disappointing and cost me my card. Several times, Mr. White asked me if I could hit the ball low? I said yes, but I was fooling myself. My shots would stay in the air too long and carry into places Lewis and Clark had not discovered, out of bounds or in a hazard.

I grew up in Hattiesburg, Mississippi, which is in a pine tree belt. Wind here amounts to almost nothing. Therefore, I never gave wind much thought, except if it was blowing hard enough for me to say, "It is too windy to play today. I did not realize that on the tour almost every tournament round has some wind—sometimes really strong! When you stop and think, golf was originally played along the seacoast, where the wind blows all the time.

The Scots like to say, "If there's nae wind, there's nae golf." Looking on this part of nature as a challenge, instead of a hindrance, is the secret to performing well.

"Bad weather and tough conditions require mental toughness and resiliency to assess this challenge and pursue it with determination and humility."—David Graham

If you have followed me this far you know with what high regard I hold the word, "determination." Perhaps no other word offers a player greater chance for success in windy conditions than his word "humility." We should all check our "egos" at the door. They have no place here. Egos offer you as much chance for success as a player trying to match par while playing "Amen Corner" with nothing but a driver.

Direct confrontation against a strong wind is plain and simple . . . dumb! Add it to your "don't want to" list. Mine includes:

1. Playing Mike Taylor at his home course at Northwood Country Club,

2. Playing Raymond Floyd *even* at Indian Creek Country Club,

3. Playing Larry Bird in a game of "horse" in the Old Boston Garden,

4. Being Mike Tyson's next opponent.

By the time I admitted my weakness, it was too late. But today I can hit it as low as anyone. I get more compliments on my wind play than any other aspect of my game. I wish Mr. White were around to see it. Like he said to his wife, "My Goodness, Mabelle, we've created a monster."

A very low drive flies best into the wind. Equally important to elevation is a well struck ball with the proper trajectory. One of the first things I did was get a driver which I could hit both high and low. Mr. White refers to this as a club that is "forgiving" or a club that is not "one way." Fortunately for me, Mr. White gave me a club that would prove to be a perfect match. Secondly, I **moved the ball back in my stance,** even as far back as across from the right toe, if needed with my iron clubs. Thirdly, I **took more club and choked down on it**. Choking down stiffens the shaft and decreases club-head speed. A 3/4, or 1/2 swing can help keep it even lower.

If possible, it is important that you hit a shot which will go from right to left—a very positive shot. This means squaring the clubhead and starting the ball to the right of the target. If the ball is played back and you have made a turn at all, this would be no problem, since the club should immediately start to the inside.

Playing in the wind will have a tendency to make a person rush his swing. Generally, I have found that the more I choked down on the club and the more I moved the ball back in my stance, the more I quickened my swing, especially the take away, and then failed to make a backswing. Be conscious of this and **remember to make a special effort to induce the right side to turn when the clubhead, hands, and arms move.** Do not just pick the club up. **There is a tendency to leave the body behind.** The more the ball is played back, the more inside the path will be and the quicker the wrist should break. Also, remember that on the down-swing the tendency is for the hands to take over, causing a lateral body move forward. Be careful, because a good hard stretch is needed through the ball.

After countless hours of practicing hitting the ball down, I can say that there is no substitute for this ability. Let me relate this story about wind play to you. It has stuck firmly in my mind and I continue to benefit from it in my decision making.

One day Mr. White, Doug, a friend of Doug's, and I were sitting around the table after finishing our play for the day. The conversation switched to wind play when Doug's friend made a comment that expressed her concern over her ability to hit the ball low. Mr. White takes such comments as a personal challenge, as though these challenges were the very reason for his getting up every morning. Immediately the four of us adjourned to the practice area. Doug and I were just observers, but we eagerly watched. As Doug's friend began hitting wedge shots, the wind picked up in the direction she was facing. Turning to Mr. White she asked, "How do you hit a low wedge?" You should be able to guess the reaction of Mr. White. Reaching into her bag, he pulled out an eight iron and handed it to her. "The way to hit a low wedge is to take an eight iron and grip it down." Thus, using a smaller swing, you let the club do the work for you. Percentage-wise this is much greater.

The girl executed well and had a half hour work out. In summary, Mr. White went back over the points he had brought out and asked if she understood or had any questions. "Yes," she said, "How do you hit a low wedge?" Both Doug and I had the same reaction. We reacted as if someone had just thrown a live grenade into where the four of us were standing. Turning away quickly and putting our fingers in our ears, we vacated the spot in anticipation of the explosion to come. I cannot put into words what came out of his mouth. Try and visualize a 68 year old man propped up against a golf bag, rattling it in an attempt to secure the right weapon. "The way to hit a low wedge," his voice quivering, "is to take an eight iron!" he exclaimed ferociously.

I have learned this lesson well. The wind is a built-in back-stop. You don't hit low wedges 99 times out of 100. You use nine irons, eight irons, and even seven irons. Muscling the ball against the wind by taking the same club and hitting it high and hard has about as much chance of becoming effective and consistent shot-making as does William Perry winning the Masters at Augusta National by getting it up and down with a sand wedge, over the back of the eighteenth green. Granted, there will be times when you will want to play a low shot and have it stop quickly (like into the wind and over a bunker), if the pin is cut close. Generally, if the wind is strong, and you are more than seventy yards away, low wedges should be low eight and nine irons.

⇐ To hit the ball low into the wind you should have the club finish out in front of you.

1987 Gasparilla Invitational

Chapter **8**

Putting

The original objective in golf—put it in the hole.

"The best system, is to go up to the ball and knock it into the hole!"—George Duncan.

"Old Man Par—he never gets down in one putt, and he never takes three."—Bobby Jones

Golf was never meant to be like this—but until it changes I guess we should harden our hearts to it. **Putting consistency calls for sensitive hands, firm footing, eyes over the ball, and a steady head position.** Regardless of choice of putters, type of stance or style of stroke you use, the most important factors are keeping the head still and hitting the putt solid. Mr. White told me something one time that shows his keen awareness. He said that in choosing a putter, choose one that does not have a lot of lines and gadgets on it. You can get too wrapped up in the putter-blade and the putter, worrying too much about being exactly lined up. Most of the great golfers have putters that are very simple looking. Such a putter will allow your mind to concentrate on the putt. Becoming too careful, trying too hard to be precise, can cause you to freeze in this address position. More often than not, this has the effect of introducing tension, making a smooth stroke impossible. Also, becoming too involved can slow you down and disturb your pattern.

Putting is very personal because it depends so much on feel and touch, rather than technique. Thinking technique, once you are over the ball, crowds your conscious mind with unnecessary thoughts. These thoughts will clog the spontaneous reaction that comes initially from your subconscious mind, thus preventing your muscles from getting an accurate read-out on how hard to hit the putt. Like the full swing, putting technique must be developed on the practice green and be second nature on the course. In reality, a putting stroke is a miniature golf swing. You must believe you can make it. Putting could be likened to shooting a basketball. You do not think of how you are going to do it, but rather visualize the ball going into the goal. Program positive thoughts. Remember the good ones and forget the bad.

There are two common putting styles. The hands-wrist method and the arms-shoulders method. Which one you use is your decision.

As I assess my past performance as a competitive golfer, I believe three things contributed to my lack of success:

1. lack of confidence (negative attitude),
2. lack of killer instinct,
3. my inability to get the ball in the hole (poor putting—32.80 strokes per round).

The best putters on the tour average 28 point something putts per round. It is hard to spot someone four strokes per round and still be competitive.

As a person who holds several course records, played nine holes in under thirty strokes six times, putted for two scores of 28, shot 30 more times than I can remember, and had countless rounds of sixty-four and better, I would lead you to assume I must be a great putter. But my inability to putt in competition had been my biggest disappointment, so in 1978 I adopted a modified version of Hubert Green's style and stuck with it for ten years.

This style helps because it is so different from the conventional way. I disassociate from any of my old negative thoughts. I move my left hand forward and use my left forearm as a brace for my forward stroke. With my right hand spread down the shaft and separate from my left about an inch, I swing the putter back and through, hitting the ball square in the back. I also have the forefinger of my right hand pointed down the shaft to add putter blade control and feel. I have found that if I bend over from the waist I increase my concentration on the ball. My feet are about a foot apart and slightly open, my weight in the middle, as well as the ball position.

As discussed earlier in the three "P's," when over the ball, this is not the time to think technique or method. I had done this all my life, and had not gotten anywhere until I learned otherwise. To disassociate from old negatives, I interpret putting the ball as—**rolling the ball**. After finding the line to putt on I say, "Just take your right hand and roll the ball along the line and into the back of the hole." It is a matter of touch and feel, the ability to gauge a slope accurately, and most important of all, the ability to concentrate on the problem at hand; that is, in your mind, seeing the ball rolling along the intended line and dropping into the hole. Be aggressive, and do not "over-read."

Place the thumbs down the shaft for better feel. In this situation, you must accelerate the clubhead or putter head toward the hole. Many golfers try to keep the putter going straight back and straight through the putt, keeping the putter blade on the line all the way. I believe this is a mistake, because it is artificial. Most good putters will let the club swing back inside naturally, then return it on the same line. Your stance is an individual thing. I do not have much to say concerning it, except to get comfortable and lock yourself in. Good putters appear to be very calm and quiet over the ball.

Keep the tempo of the stroke smooth and unhurried, hands ahead of the blade. As you go through the ball, do not attempt to lift the putter blade. **A good solid rap in the back of the ball is all that is needed** to cause overspin. Overspin will tend to make the putt roll truer. Try to putt over a spot. Visualize the ball rolling along the intended line and into the hole. Concentrate on the positive. Learn the sweet spot in your putter and try to give the ball a "solid rap." One of the terms that helped me was, "box your putts," especially the short ones, as Mr. White called it. This means to pop the ball solid into the back of the hole. The legendary Walter Travis, reportedly one of the greatest putters the game has ever known, always said that he visualized the putting stroke as an attempt to drive an imaginary tack into the back of the ball.

One day, while playing with Mr. White, Bug "Cap" Thames, Gary Cooper, and Garrard White, I asked Mr. White what he thought about Bug. He said, "I was impressed about one thing in particular. Once he made up his mind, he went right ahead with it. It was apparent that he wasn't think-ing about the next one." Mr. White was referring to Bug's play on the greens. If memory serves me right, Bug did man-age a 69.

Your routine in putting should be to look over the putt to the best of your ability and as fast as you can; then decide what the putt is going to do and do not change your mind. Don't second guess yourself. Your first impression is usually right. "Over-reading" was one of my biggest faults. Staying behind the ball too long and looking for every single thing can only be harmful. Concern yourself with the more general contours of a slope, rather than to try and account for every little hop or roll the ball is likely to take. "I believe that bad putting is due more to the effect the green has upon the player than that it has upon the action of the ball."–Bobby Jones Use your three "P's."

Remember, you either make or miss. I am still working on this. Visualize what you want the ball to do. Be confident that you have chosen the right path. Then walk up and hit it. "There's the hole, here's the ball—now go," is what Mr. White told me. "The best system is to go up to the ball and knock it into the hole!"–George Duncan Repeating—the original objective in golf is to put the ball in the hole.

I do most of my practice strokes away from the ball. I think "analysis breeds paralysis" when you're getting ready to putt. Poor putters putt too slowly and invite paralysis. When you feel some tension creeping in, before you make the putt, it is best that you admit it to yourself and do something about it. I like to think that being nervous adds adrenalin to help you accomplish your goal. Nothing is wrong. So realize it and do your best. Also, I find it helpful to ball my hands into fists, then spread my fingers very wide apart, extending them as far as I can. I then relax them. I roll my head around and try to loosen my neck and shoulders. I also make it a point to stand a little taller. Many golfers put extra pressure on by telling themselves they have to make certain putts. The truth is that a putt cannot be successfully steered no more than any other golf shot. **You either make or miss,** as I said before. One secret is to accept each putt at face value (one stroke). You can't control what happens after the ball leaves the putter face. Hit the putt as well as you can, and do not allow any worry over the possible outcome to spoil the stroke. Play shot-for-shot. Never carry a shot over to the next one.

The main considerations in planning a putt are the terrain and the breaks in the green. Study the slope to determine which way your ball is going to roll. The way the green slopes is, obviously, the way your ball if going to break. If it is a subtle slope, it helps to take a look at the entire green and determine where the low spots are, in order to see which way the water drains off. It is also vital to figure out the final break around the hole so you can allow for this when the ball slows down. Visualize the entire path to the cup and the drop into the cup.

If you die your putt at the hole, you may have a greater chance of making it. The speed varies, depending on the surface of the greens and the types of grasses. To overcome the effect of imperfections on the green, the ball must be struck harder and rolled faster. Once the ball slows, these hidden bumps turn the ball off line. The ball must be struck the hardest on Bermuda grass .

Walter Hagen said, "Short putts are missed because it is not physically possible to make the little ball travel over uncertain ground for three or four feet with any degree of regularity.

It is far better that we count missed putts as part of the game, and leave our minds free and open to make others, without the suggestion entering the head that our putting stroke is all wrong." I am sure all of us have been guilty of this. I have marveled at the confidence of some people with whom I have played. They seem to make everything. I can assure you that everyone of them have drilled the ball into the back of the hole. Not only does this indicate a solidly struck putt, but also confidence and aggressiveness.

"But you see, **putting is want.** He wanted to get the ball in the hole. Physically, it's almost impossible to take that putter back and role the ball over all that terrain and into that little hole from any distance. **But want, that is somthing else."**

—Ivan Gantz

Four essential qualities of good putting are:
(1) hands slightly forward of the ball at address,
(2) eyes aligned directly over the ball,
(3 & 4) a still body and a quiet head position during the stroke.

Chapter **9**

Tempo & Rhythm

A necessary evil under pressure.

After winning his first Masters title in 1977, Tom Watson said, "When I learned how to breathe, I learned how to win."

What is tempo?

How would you define tempo?

We all know when we see someone who has it. Likewise, we know when we see someone who does not have it. Repeating, the golf swing is best performed in a correct sequence of movements and this sequence is the best way to obtain tempo.

Tempo is the ability to make different muscles work together in an orderly fashion so that the rhythm is unhurried, smooth, and continuous from start to finish. Since each shot in golf is played from a start, it is important to establish peace of mind, have inner rhythm, and remain faithful at all times. If you alter the rhythm, you are sure to destroy the inner peace that helps you swing smoothly and decisively.

The cure for this is to work on your pre-shot routine and use it on every swing, regardless of whether you are practicing or playing tournaments. Pressure doesn't change the demands of playing a shot, so why change your approach to hitting it?

Webster's dictionary defines tempo as: the rate of speed at which a muscular composition is, or is supposed to be played. As a golfer I am not interested in defining tempo. I want to know how to obtain it. Timing then is:

1. The gathering of speed through the ball from correct mechanical movement,

2. A correct location of the swing center.

It might be said that we have timed a shot well only when we feel we have stayed a long time in contact with the ball. Have you ever heard anyone say, "my timing's off?"

One of the funniest lines Mabelle White ever told me was pertaining to her standard answer when confronted by different players in Buck's absence. Golfers are a desperate breed and confiding in Mrs. White as to their problems implies knowledge by association. Her remark was one that satisfied them for the time being and sent them on their way. As Mrs. White told me before, "David, I'd like to listen, but I'm all booked up through Christmas."

"You'll be all right, your timing is just off." was Mrs. White's reply. Saying your timing is off is OK in jest, but it doesn't suggest how to get your timing back. More often than not, this is just an excuse by unknowable people.

Rhythm is a flowing motion, and in golf this translates itself into timed movements. The best definition I know is: "coordination of mind and muscle which enables the player to do exactly the right thing at the right moment." You must find your own rhythm. The rhythm with which the swing takes place differs with each individual—some slow, some not so slow. Physiques and temperaments are two big factors.

During the fall qualifying tour school at Disney World in 1975 my friend and caddy, Doug Taylor, and I hit upon some words that stick in my mind. These three words helped greatly to relax me. They were:

- ☞ **long**
- ☞ **slow**
- ☞ **smooth**

Also remember:

- ☞ **Light grip pressure**
- ☞ **Complete the backswing**
- ☞ **Trust your swing**
- ☞ **Plan effectively**
- ☞ **Relax (breathe deep)**
- ☞ **Correct sequence of movements**
  (See chapter on swing).

Chapter **10**

Golf Clubs

"You know that won't work, Mr. White."

"I don't know until I try it, David. After all, how else do I fight senility?"

According to Mr. White, the modern day golfer has neglected his education of golf clubs. I've spent much time with him learning different designs and characteristics. A good player, one who has mastered the techniques, is still only as good as his equipment. While there are currently many fine clubs on the market, that has not always been the case.

In 1964, at age fourteen, I was an eager young golfer at the Hattiesburg Country Club. The assistant pro was Freddie Leffingwell. Freddie was fresh off the tour, and a former Florida State University player and 1955 National Junior Champion. Through Freddie I had my first experiences in club repair. I remember the first set of clubs I worked on. I had re-gripped a set of clubs for a man from out of town. About a week later this same man returned with his clubs. The grips I had put on were all crooked. The club shafts were undersized shafts and I had forgotten to use two rolls of tape to build up the grips. What a start for me! I soon corrected my faults and moved on to bigger and better things. Next on the list was mastering the art of wrapping clubs. This gave me no problem, even though stopping and starting can at times be troublesome.

Learning about swing weight, overall weight, and flex of shafts is not difficult. Next came repairs like reshafting, replacing inserts, changing weights, and refinishing clubs. The golfer need not be an expert in club repair, but an overall understanding is mandatory. Someone may not always be around to fix your clubs.

My education on golf clubs continued with my first class under Mr. White. He examined every club in my bag. He picked my brain to determine my knowledge of clubs. Included in my education was the history of golf clubs, and how to use them. I stuck my foot in my mouth again when I complained to Mr. White about laminated woods. He said, "Where do you hit the ball, David, in the woods or the insert?" I no longer worry about woods—I go around feeling inserts.

Once a man stopped to investigate the noise coming from a back room at the Sea Course in Biloxi where Mr. White was busy altering a set of clubs to specification. Setting foot in the door, the man said sarcastically, "Do you know what you're doing?" "I sure hope so!" came the indignant reply. Mr. White had been doing this for more than fifty years. Though he did not know it, this stranger was also talking to a man who could tell how many degrees a club had just by eyeballing. Another day, while accompanying Mr. White into a golf shop, I casually picked up a wood to examine it and remarked about my dissatisfaction with the club. "Don't say you don't like it. Say it can be fixed!" he retorted.

I would like to point out those things that a golfer needs to know about his equipment so that he does not always have to depend on others.

1. In irons, two important factors are cambering, and the leading edge out in front and rolled.

2. In woods, facing is a must. This is important because manufacturers are hesitant to spend the time due to the cost factor. It is also costly. My driver has an exaggerated four-way role on the face. It also has 8, 9, and 10 degrees loft. Good characteristics are small neck, no crown, and no needless overhang.

Imagine someone looking for a work bench to set up shop with only a bending tool and a lead hammer that dates back to the 1930's. Mr. White carried these in the trunk of his car; and according to Mrs. White, this was the reason they did not fly when making an annual pilgrimage to Florida . . ."You never know when you might need to set-up shop!"

TRAINING

Fame never yet found a man who waited to be found. Most of our troubles are caused by too much bone in the head, and not enough in the back.

Training is essential in every sport and golf is no exception, especially if you are an aspiring young golfer as I once was. The first step in training is to plan a program. Then, make an unbiased evaluation of where you are and where you want to go. Where you are now will determine where you start. In order not to leave anyone out, I will first direct my thoughts to a youngster or beginner.

Begin by learning the fundamentals of the golf swing. Learn the rules, become competitive, enjoying yourself; and be a well-rounded athlete, Do not committ to golf as the only sport when young.

In retrospect, as a youngster one of the best things I had was a hero. He was Mike Taylor of Meridian, Mississippi, a former All-American at Brigham Young University and the same Mike Taylor Johnny Miller wrote about in his book, *Pure Golf*. Mike was ten-times a State Amateur Champion and also a student of Mr. White. Mike was my All-Everything—the person I looked up to. The one I enjoyed being with. (I caddied for many good golfers.)

I stress the importance of practicing. I do not mean just hitting balls. Do not make the mistake of seeing how far you can hit the ball. I did not hit many balls and seldom, if ever, practiced chipping and putting. The way you win in golf is by shooting the lowest score. I know it is an asset to hit the ball far, but the best putter will win every time.

The Bible says, *For what does it profit a man if he gains the whole world and loses his soul* (Mark 8:36). Likewise, what does it profit a golfer if he gains distance at the expense of putting. What good does it do to hit it far if you cannot keep it in play. As I stated earlier, the leading money winners average between 28 and 30 putts per round. If you do not have a desire to culitvate the ability to putt close to these numbers, especially if you have tour aspirations, perhaps you should find another sport. My average on tour was 32.80. I averaged .715% greens. Around .720% usually leads the PGA tour.

I now direct my attention to the intermediate golfer. This person is either a high school or collegiate golfer. By this time, overall physical fitness should be very much a part of your life. A correct evaluation of where you are is extremely important.

The following list is important to the intermediate player in order to continue his training program in the evolution of a golfer:

1. Enter competitive events.
   Play in as many tournaments as possible.
   There is no substitution for tournament experience.
   One of my biggest drawbacks was a lack of competition.

2. Attend tour events. This will go a long way in creating enthusiasm.

3. Notice and observe tour pros.

4. Find a good teacher and good books.

5. Have a set of good clubs.

6. Practice and more practice.

7. Caddy in tour events.

Let's move to the collegiate and young tour player. By now, this person should have a good understanding of himself and his game. What is needed is to continue improving technique and increasing knowledge of golf clubs. I remember a conversation I had with Mr. White. We were discussing whether or not Spalding could make the set of clubs I wanted. Mr. White said, "They can if you can tell them what it is you want." My ability to communicate with the man in the custom orders department determined whether or not I received the clubs I needed. Many golfers know what they like when they see it, but cannot convey it to anyone else.

You already know that a correct evaluation of your golf game and practice, practice, and more practice is a must for improvement. How do you evaluate correctly, and what do you practice. One of the best things that ever happened to me was Mr. White making it mandatory that I keep notes of my lessons and to write down information about every round. I had to keep a ledger of all my competitive rounds. This included:

1. What I shot.
2. Weather conditions.
3. Where I played and with whom.
4. General comments about the round (happenings and penalty strokes, etc.)
5. Every hole—what I hit, where it went, how far from the hole it was (left, right, short or long).
6. How many putts.
7. Percentage of ups and downs.
8. Fairway hits.
9. How many greens in regulation I hit.

By keeping a ledger, you will take all the guesswork out of your evaluation and you will know what to practice.

EXERCISE

Warming up is important before practicing. Start slow and work up. It is important to gain confidence. Many times I swing a weighted club or even two clubs. One exercise I have found to be good is to take my position, swing back by stretching to the top, and hold for a few seconds. After doing this a few times I will be panting. Good physical condition is important to playing good golf; so exercise regularly and stay fit. Running and jogging are helpful. Distance running can help build mental toughness and confidence. It also gives some time to think back over your rounds.

I recommend very light hand weights for exercise; many stretching exercises—hanging, bending and other calisthenics.

A golfer is like a chain—no stronger than the weakest link. The hands are the weak link of every golfer, no matter how strong his hands may be. The hand must maintain control of the club throughout the swing and be strong enough to absorb the shock during impact.

I recommend that you have all the hand strength that is possible for you to acquire. A grip developer will help in strengthening grip.

Physical strength and conditioning do count for something in golf. The person who generates the greatest clubhead speed will achieve the longest drive. Rhythm, timing, and the other essentials of form add to this player's ability.

One night I telephoned Mr. White. Mabelle answered and said that I should call back at nine o'clock because he was swinging his club. Since it was about seven o'clock, I thought it strange that I must wait until nine. When I called back, Mr. White came to the phone panting like dog.

"Hello, David," he said.

"What on earth have you been doing since I phoned earlier?" I asked.

"Swinging my club," he replied.

"Swinging your club?" I said.

"Yes David, 500 times a night. After all, you do what you have to do to play, and I do what I have to do to play." It is no wonder that, at such a late age in life, Mr. White could walk and carry his bag, not to mention that it was very rare for him to shoot over par.

Sam Snead was once asked to what did he most contribute to his lasting career. He said, "For as long as I played golf, I have never laid off for more than a few days at a time."

PRACTICE

A sure way to gain confidence is by experiencing success, and the only way to experience success is to practice. Failure should be a stimuli for success, not discouragement. Success should be a stimuli for perfection, not satisfaction. Practice will bring you a hundred virtues which the idle will never know.

"By innumerable repetitions, habits will be formed. It is the reward of the patient and persevering." –Seymour Dunn

The first thing a golfer must learn on the road to success is that practicing is not merely hitting balls, but rather what you get out of what you hit. Often I hear someone say, "I hit three-hundred balls today," or "I have practiced for three hours." This is well and good, but what has been gained? Be constructive in your work. Have a specific objective in mind before you start. Remember, golf is like football and good football is blocking and tackling. Master the fundamentals. When trouble arises, one piece of advice that has been proven more valuable than anything else is "go back to basics." Mr. White and I have started many sessions this way. Play like you practice—go through your routine and your three "P's" on every shot. Planning, pattern and position are essential for good golf and good practice. Give total! If you cannot give every shot your all—walk away.

"Golf is an art requiring such marvelous dexterity of touch, that to excel, extremely accurate judgment in touch is necessary."–Seymour Dunn

Good judgment and proper touch are things which can be developed only with a great deal of practice. The player must practice along proper lines in order to acquire a good sense of judgment in touch. Mr. White said, "Practice doesn't make perfect. Perfect practice makes perfect."

Here is a short story with a powerful message.

Once upon a time in a land far, far away lived a young boy and a young girl. As they grew up, they fell in love, and at the right time became husband and wife. This young man had a strong back and **worked many long hours.** He got up early and went to bed late. **He was not a lazy man.** Each day he was **well prepared** to meet life's challenges with a **zest for life and enthusiasm.** He was **not easily discouraged** although he suffered many setbacks. Failure was not a part of his vocabulary, because he was **willing to sacrifice much to obtain his goal**. He was a trusted man and had peace of mind because he **exhibited fair play** in all of his dealings. Among his list of virtues was **desire,** for once he started something he was **determined** to see it through. His name was **Proper.**

The wife patiently waited for her husband to return at the end of each day. This lady was easy to talk with because she **listened so attentively.** She took such **pride** in her appearance and **displayed a wonderful temperament,** that her husband could not wait to show her off. You could tell by looking at her that she **had great poise,** because of the way she carried herself. She **walked tall,** her head up, and **knew where she was going.** She **visualized herself successful,** and was not satisfied with anything else. Among her virtues was **wisdom,** because she was **slow to anger.** Her name was **Practice.**

One day the couple received a great blessing; a child was born to them. They named him **Confidence.**

The moral to this story is: **Confidence is born of proper practice.**

Today we live in a world where cameras and visual equipment have become very much a part of the game of golf. These have proven to be excellent teaching aids. Useful as they are, I have found a mirror and my shadow to be a close companion. I have often been kidded about standing in front of mirrors so long. A mirror will help you see yourself and help you visualize mental pictures. In actual playing conditions, the player cannot see himself. He must play and adjust his swing wholly to feel. He has no other guide than the sensations produced by the action of his muscles.

Here are some thoughts that have helped me in practicing:

"There can be no progress, no achievement, without sacrifice. He who would accomplish little need sacrifice little, but he who would achieve much need sacrifice much."

Love not sleep, lest thou come to poverty, open thine eyes, and thou shalt be satisfied with bread (Proverbs 20:13).

For a just man falleth seven times, and riseth up again; but the wicked shall fall into mischief (Proverbs 24:16).

Don't stop if you are not successful the first time. Remember: *In all labor there is profit* (Proverbs 14:2).

"No virtue in this world is so often rewarded as perseverance."

When taking lessons, first check your teacher's background. To my knowledge, there have never been any good teachers who are not good players. I do not mean to imply that all good players are good teachers. This is not true. Good players need not excel in any category, although they may. As we have discovered, Mr. Hogan said that good swings do not win tournaments, good management does. Mr. Nicklaus said that desire was the greatest quality, and Mr. Jones said he did not really learn how to win until he learned his real adversary was Old Man Par.

Teachers, like players, may not excel in all categories. A teacher may have a good working knowledge of the basic mechanics of a golf swing and know little about putting and chipping. He may be proficient in putting and chipping and not be able to properly strike a golf ball or tell someone else how. Mr. White's only comment to me on putting, outside of boxing my putts, was to go up to George Low and offer him $100 to watch me hit a few putts. Good teachers must be able to communicate and have a desire to help people, two characteristics a good player need not have. A good way to rate golf instructors is to think of them as school teachers. Teachers, depending on their training, knowledge, experience and ability, may be on any appropriate grade level. Golf instructors are no different. Who did he learn from? Are there any great golfers who do what he says? Who has he taught? These are good questions you should when choosing a teacher. Use common sense. Don't be fooled.

It is better to hear the rebuke of the wise, than to hear the song of fools (Ecclesiastes. 7:5).

Practice all types of shots in all sorts of situations—even out of water. I am sure Nicklaus does. Mr. White told me, "The more you practice the luckier you get." Remember, in taking lessons and playing golf, that change is a must for improving, and "looks don't count." It is a game of constant change and adjustments. Some golfers are worried about how they look. What they should be concerned with is, "does it work?" Practicing and playing go hand-in-hand. When in a tournament it is time to forget everything else, time to leave off experimenting, and time to completely trust in the muscular habits you have acquired through constant repetition. Concentrate on getting the ball in the hole. In most situations where I have performed poorly, I knew it was my own lack of preparation or bad thinking that led to my demise. **"Failure exists only in the grave. Man, being alive, hath not yet failed; always he may turn about and ascend by the same path he descended by."** –Frederick Day

If that does not give you hope and confidence for tomorrow, maybe this will. You could make a strong argument for Bobby Jones being the greatest golfer of all times. His achievements are legendary. Yet, Mr. Jones was quoted as saying, "There are times when I feel I know less about what I am doing than anybody else in the world." A sobering statement coming from the only person ever to win golf's "grand slam." If there are nights that you go to sleep feeling you do not have all the answers to life's questions—sleep soundly, you are in good company.

"There's still a little daylight left; so let's get with it. **After all David, you haven't failed . . . you just haven't suc-ceeded.**"—Buck White

In Conclusion

In 1990, having returned to pro golf, David Smith set his sights on returning to the PGA Tour.

First he made a comprehensive review of the fundamentals, and of the notes left to him by Mr. Buck White. This was followed by a return to a full competitive schedule of local and state tournaments, as well as an occasional Ben Hogan event or an attempt to qualify for a PGA tournament.

The first year was marked with occasional successes, but no wins. Failing to regain his PGA card, and successfuly negotiating the first stage of tour school but faltering down the stretch in the second stage, a disappointed David returned home.

Analyzing his play, it seemed that he had played well from tee to green only to record a much higher score each day. Whether he blamed his putting or that he got in his own way, the sad conclusion was that David needed to return to the drawing board with new dedication.

1992 began much the same as 1991. Five months of practice, then playing in competition. Again, David's performance was no better than the previous year. Some success, some good golf, hard work, and a lack of consistency resulting in no wins. After again analyzing his performance, and reviewing his notes, and working on all aspects of the game with no results, David came to the realization that he had been relying on his own merits to get the job done. He realized that he could accomplish nothing without God's help. David decided to do what he could and leave the rest to God.

In June, 1992 David played in seven events which included twelve rounds of golf. The result was a a collective 51 under par, including three straight wins. David's first win (Windermere Country Club, Orlando), was highlighted by an opening round nine under par 63 which saw a course record 28 on the back nine.

The newspapers rang out praises to David Smith. Then, there was another downturn. In the next three tournaments David didn't place "in the money." Remembering his "promises," the following week he returned to a winner's circle to repeat his performance twice: followed by another win in the next event, then another, and yet another—again in a fifth straight and record-setting event. (Ten more rounds of golf 39 under par.)

The moral of the story is that you can "flip" the coin, but Almighty God determines whether it comes up "heads" or "tails."

Bibliography

Jones, Bobby, *Bobby Jones on Golf*, New York: Metropolitan Fiction Co., 1930

Jones, Bobby and O.B. Keeler, *Down the Fairway*, New York: Minton Balch & Co., 1927

Barkow, Al, *Gettin' To The Dance Floor*, New York, Atheneum, 1986

Dunn, Seymour, *Golf Fundamentals*, Norwalk. Reprint 1984 by Golf Digest, Inc.

Nicklaus, Jack, *Golf My Way*, New York: Simon and Schuster, 1974

King James Version, *The Holy Bible*, World

Armour, Tommy, *How to Play Your Best Golf All the Time*, New York: Simon and Schuster

Graham, David, *Mental Toughness Training for Golf*, Pelham Books, 1990

Aultman, Dick and Ken Bowden, *The Methods of Golf's Masters, New York:Coward McCann and Geoghegan, Inc., 1975*

Hogan, Ben, *The Modern Fundamentals of Golf*, New York: A.S. Barnes and Co., 1957

Boomer, Percy, *On Learning Golf*, New York: Knopf, 1946

Blumenson, Martin Patton, *The Man Behind the Legend, 1885-1945, New York: William Morrow and Company, Inc., 1985*

Peale, Norman Vincent, *The Power of Positive Thinking*, A Fawcett Crest Book, 1956

Maltz, Maxwell, *Psycho-Cybernetics*, New York: Simon and Schuster, 1960

Miller, Johnny, *Pure Golf*, New York: Doubleday & Co., 1976

Schuller, Robert, *Tough Times Never Last, But Tough People Do! New York: Bantam Books, 1984*

Mandino, O.G., *University of Success*, New York: Bantam Books, 1982

Province, Charles M., *The Unknown Patton*, Bonanza Books, 1983

Books by Starburst Publishers

(Partial listing—full list available on request)

Dr. Kaplan's Lifestyle of the Fit & Famous   —Eric Scott Kaplan

Subtitled: *A Wellness Approach to "Thinning and Winning."* A comprehensive guide to the formulas and principles of: FAT LOSS, EXERCISE, VITAMINS, NATURAL HEALTH, SUCCESS and HAPPINESS. More than a health book—it is a lifestyle based on the empirical formulas of healthy living. Dr. Kaplan's food-combining principles take into account all the major food sources (fats, proteins, carbohydrates, sugars, etc.) that when combined within the proper formula (e.g. proteins cannot be mixed with refined carbohydrates) will increase metabolism and decrease the waistline. This allows you to eat the foods you want, feel great, and eliminate craving and binging.

(hardcover) ISBN 091498456X **$21.95**

Common Sense Management & Motivation   —Roy H. Holmes

Teaches the principles of motivating subordinate personnel via good human relations, It is written from practical "how-to" experience rather than classroom theory. Specific subjects covered include: Basic motivation psychology, Effective communication, Delegating, Goal-setting, Confronting, and Leadership qualities. A must book for all existing or aspiring supervisors, managers, business leaders, and anyone else interested in managing and motivating people.

(hardcover) ISBN 0914984497 **$16.95**

Lease–Purchase America!   —John Ross

A first-of-its-kind book that provides a simple "nuts and bolts" approach to acquiring real estate. Explains how the lease-purchase technique pioneered by John Ross can now be used in real estate to more easily buy and sell a home. Details the value of John's technique from the perspective of each participant in the real estate transaction. Illustrates how the reader can use lease-purchase successfully as a tool to achieve his or her real estate goals.

(trade paper) ISBN 0914984454 **$9.95**

Purchasing Information

Listed books are available from your favorite Bookstore, either from current stock or special order. To assist bookstore in locating your selection be sure to give title, author, and ISBN #. If unable to purchase from the bookstore you may order direct from STARBURST PUBLISHERS. When ordering enclose full payment plus $2.50 for shipping and handling ($3.00 if Canada or Overseas). Payment in US Funds only. Please allow two to three weeks minimum (longer overseas) for delivery. Make checks payable to and mail to STARBURST PUBLISHERS, P.O. Box 4123, LANCASTER, PA 17604. Credit card orders may also be placed by calling 1-800-441-1456 (credit card orders only), Mon-Fri, 8 AM-5 PM Eastern Time. **Prices subject to change without notice.**

04-95